Operations Management Cases

The McGraw-Hill/Irwin Series in Operations and Decision Sciences

Operations Management Cases

William V. Gehrlein
University of Delaware

McGraw-Hill
Irwin

Boston   Burr Ridge, IL   Dubuque, IA   Madison, WI   New York   San Francisco   St. Louis
Bangkok   Bogotá   Caracas   Kuala Lumpur   Lisbon   London   Madrid   Mexico City
Milan   Montreal   New Delhi   Santiago   Seoul   Singapore   Sydney   Taipei   Toronto

McGraw-Hill
Irwin

OPERATIONS MANAGEMENT CASES
Published by McGraw-Hill/Irwin, a business unit of The McGraw-Hill Companies, Inc., 1221 Avenue of the Americas, New York, NY, 10020. Copyright © 2005 by The McGraw-Hill Companies, Inc. All rights reserved. No part of this publication may be reproduced or distributed in any form or by any means, or stored in a database or retrieval system, without the prior written consent of The McGraw-Hill Companies, Inc., including, but not limited to, in any network or other electronic storage or transmission, or broadcast for distance learning.
Some ancillaries, including electronic and print components, may not be available to customers outside the United States.

This book is printed on acid-free paper.

2 3 4 5 6 7 8 9 0 DOC/DOC 0 9 8 7 6 5

ISBN 0-07-291866-7

Vice president and editor-in-chief: *Robin J. Zwettler*
Editorial director: *Brent Gordon*
Executive editor: *Richard T. Hercher, Jr.*
Editorial assistant: *Lee Stone*
Marketing manager: *Greta Kleinert*
Project manager: *Marlena Pechan*
Production supervisor: *Gina Hangos*
Designer: *Kami Carter*
Supplement producer: *Lynn M. Bluhm*
Senior digital content specialist: *Brian Nacik*
Cover design: *Kami Carter*
Typeface: *10.5/12 Times New Roman*
Compositor: *GAC Indianapolis*
Printer: *R. R. Donnelley*

Library of Congress Cataloging-in-Publication Data

Gehrlein, William V.
    Operations management cases / William V. Gehrlein.
        p. cm. — (McGraw-Hill/Irwin series Operations and decision sciences)
    ISBN 0-07-291866-7 (alk. paper)
    1. Production management—Case studies. 2. Industrial management—Case studies.
I. Title II. Series.
TS155.G3645 2005
658.5—dc22

2003064857

www.mhhe.com

Acknowledgements

This collection of cases has evolved over many years of teaching operations management. Students in these courses have suggested many of the ideas in these cases in various ways. These suggestions have sometimes come from having a project group come up with a reasonable, but different, interpretation of a case than the one that was originally intended. Sometimes the suggestions have come from students, and other randomly met individuals, who simply enjoy talking about how they do things where they work. There was also a lot of input from many students who worked on the original versions of these cases, before some of the bugs had been worked out of them. I am grateful to them, particularly to the ones who developed a serious interest in this material and made it fun to be in class.

Gratitude is also extended to those who reviewed the initial draft for this book and provided helpful suggestions. These reviewers include Seung-Lae Kim (Drexel University), Stephen Mumford (Gwynned-Mercy College), V. Udayabhanu (San Francisco State University), Geoff Willis (University of Central Oklahoma), Zinovy Radovilsky (California State University–Hayward), Zubair Mohamed (Western Kentucky University), and Ramachandran Natarajan (Tennessee Technological University).

Other individuals have been helpful along the way by continuously offering encouragement to complete not only this project, but others too. The notable standouts in this group of people include Barbara E. Eller, Burton A. Abrams, and Arthur A. Sloane.

William V. Gehrlein

To the memory of Vincent F. and Eunice K. Gehrlein.

Table of Contents

Forecasting

Noyes Rain Gear, Ltd.

Noyes Rain Gear, Ltd. (NRG), is a firm that produces a large number of different items that are related to foul-weather clothing and associated paraphernalia, such as umbrellas, waterproof ponchos, and rain suits. The firm is looking for a simple and reasonably accurate forecasting technique to develop short-term predictions of demand for each of its products. Simple exponential smoothing (SES) is being considered as a tool for that purpose. In order to test the efficacy of using SES, a sample product has been selected from NRG's line. Quarterly actual demand for this product over the past five years is shown in Exhibit 1.1, and there is some obvious seasonality in the pattern of demand for this particular product. Seasonality effects in the demand for products of this type are clearly something that should be expected. The data set that is shown in Exhibit 1.1 represents 20 consecutive quarters of demand data, starting in Q1 of Year 1 and ending in Q4 of Year 5. Since the goal is to consider only simple forecasting techniques, seasonal indexes should be obtained from the proportions of quarterly sales, accumulated over the entire five years of demand values that are available.

The manager of NRG wants to use a forecasting technique that is the most accurate on an overall basis, based on its performance on the trial data set. Forecast accuracy should be measured in terms of how well the actual quarterly sales values compare to the seasonalized quarterly forecasts, with the overall forecasting error being measured by the average amount that forecasts and actual demands differ. NRG management has not expressed any particular concerns as to whether demand forecasts tend to be over, or under, their respective actual quarterly demands. As a result, we should measure forecast accuracy based on the magnitude, or absolute value, of the seasonalized forecast error.

The demand values for the four quarters in Year 1 are needed as part of the data for getting the seasonal indexes and to get an initial quarterly forecast to start forecasting

EXHIBIT 1.1
Quarterly Demand for a Representative NRG Product

Quarter	Year 1	Year 2	Year 3	Year 4	Year 5
Q1	145,400	152,000	147,500	152,600	165,000
Q2	173,200	168,000	171,600	186,440	181,900
Q3	82,000	87,200	104,400	104,100	105,000
Q4	115,600	143,000	134,300	137,800	134,900

with SES. SES should only be used on deseasonalized data, so some initial deseasonalized forecast must be estimated. This initial deseasonalized forecast will be for Q3 of Year 1, and it should be obtained as the average deseasonalized demand for the first three quarters of Year 1. SES is then used to obtain the first real deseasonalized quarterly forecast for Q4 of Year 1. Seasonality should then be brought back into the forecasting technique after the deseasonalized SES forecasts have been obtained. Since there are no real seasonalized forecasts for Q1, Q2, and Q3 of Year 1, these quarters should be ignored when determining the average absolute seasonalized forecast error.

The manager of NRG wants to see some specific output from this project. A specification of the α value, from the possible $\alpha = 0, .1, .2, .3, \ldots, .9, 1.0$ values, that should be used with SES to minimize the average absolute seasonalized forecast error is of primary interest. In order to estimate the sensitivity of the selection of this particular α, it is also of interest to see a plot of the average absolute forecast error over the range of values $\alpha = 0, .1, .2, .3, \ldots, .9, 1.0$, with an explanation of any particular patterns that are observed in this plot. Once the specific α value has been found that tends to be most accurate over the given data set, two other things are desired. First, we want the forecast that would be obtained for Q1 of Year 6. Second, some evidence of how these forecasts are working, with the selected α, should be provided. This can be done by developing a plot that shows the 17 relevant quarterly demand values from Q4 of Year 1 through Q4 of Year 5, along with the 17 associated seasonalized forecasts that would have been obtained with the α that has been selected. Comments about the overall performance of the selected forecasting technique, based on observations from this plot, will be helpful to the evaluation.

Garciaparra Sports Equipment

Garciaparra Sports Equipment (GSE) is an international distributor of equipment for all types of sports. The firm distributes equipment in many different countries, primarily in North and South America. GSE is interested in developing a forecasting technique to give reasonable forecasts for each of its many different product lines. A representative product has been chosen as a test case to evaluate some simple forecasting techniques. This particular product was selected as a test case because its demand is highly seasonal, and the seasonality also has an unusual pattern, making it a difficult product for forecasting demand.

This particular product is one of many items that GSE carries that are used when playing baseball. There is a fairly steady demand for most baseball-related products from locations with climates such that the game can be played on a year-round basis. Demand tends to have a significant increase during late spring and summer, when baseball can be played in less temperate climates like the northeastern part of the United States. There is also a peak in demand in December when these items are purchased as Christmas gifts. Monthly demand for this representative product for the past four years is given in Exhibit 2.1.

EXHIBIT 2.1
Monthly Demand for the Representative Product from GSE Sales Records

	Year 1	Year 2	Year 3	Year 4
January	11,006	16,870	21,515	26,779
February	13,198	19,288	23,341	28,897
March	12,776	19,393	23,778	27,935
April	14,216	18,428	24,105	31,554
May	18,523	24,444	28,468	33,909
June	22,800	27,728	35,109	39,742
July	21,302	26,846	30,760	40,586
August	16,511	24,310	31,828	33,102
September	14,954	20,337	28,907	34,268
October	11,173	18,309	27,399	29,339
November	11,066	14,480	21,830	27,125
December	16,449	20,233	28,060	31,984

The management of GSE only wants to consider the use of simple forecasting techniques for each product, since they carry thousands of different lines of sporting goods. As a result, attention will be limited to forecasting with moving averages. There is an obvious seasonality that is associated with this particular product, and it must be accounted for in the forecasts. To keep things simple, seasonal indexes should be derived from the overall proportions of monthly demand, accumulated over the entire four years' worth of data.

The primary concern is the determination of the number of periods, k, that should be used in the moving-averages forecast. The objective is to find a forecasting technique that is the most accurate on an overall basis. Forecast accuracy is relevant in terms of how well the actual monthly sales values compare to the seasonalized monthly forecasts. Forecasting error should be measured by the average amount that forecasts and actual demands differ. No concerns have been expressed as to whether forecasts tend to be over, or under, true monthly demands. The only interest is in the magnitude, or absolute value, of the forecast error.

In order to obtain a fair comparison of how accurate the forecasts are with different k values, we will compare all different forecasts that would have been obtained when using $k = 1, 2, 3, \ldots, 12$ by testing them against the data set for the sequence of 36 consecutive monthly demands from January of Year 2 through December of Year 4. The demand values for the 12 months in Year 1 are needed as part of the data for getting the monthly seasonal indexes and to get the initial monthly forecasts in Year 2. However, no forecasts should be obtained for any month in Year 1.

The manager of GSE wants to see some specific analysis from this project. The manager wants to know which k value to use to minimize the average absolute forecast error. In addition, it is of interest to see a table of the average absolute forecast error over the range of values $k = 1, 2, 3, \ldots, 12$, with an explanation of any particular patterns that are observed in this table. Once the k has been found that tends to be most accurate, two other things are of interest. First, we want the forecast that would be obtained for January of Year 5. Second, some evidence of how these forecasts are working, with the selected k, should be provided. This can be done by developing a plot that shows the 36 monthly demand values from January of Year 2 through December of Year 4, along with the 36 associated forecasts that would have been obtained with the k that has been selected.

J. F. Mamjjasond, Inc.

J. F. Mamjjasond, Inc. (JFM) is a large firm that owns a chain of retail outlets that are located throughout the northern mid-western states, mostly in Minnesota and Wisconsin. The stores carry numerous different types of products, and the firm is interested in developing a simple short-term forecasting model to give reasonably accurate estimates of monthly demand for each of the thousands of different items that it keeps in stock. In order to establish an idea of how effective some basic forecasting techniques might be at predicting short-term demand for these products, a sample product has been selected for analysis. This particular product was intentionally selected as a difficult test for the possible forecasting techniques, since it has both a highly significant seasonality component and a highly significant pattern of growth in its demand. Monthly demand for this particular product for the past three years is given in Exhibit 3.1. These monthly demand values represent 36 consecutive monthly values, starting in January of Year 1 and ending in December of Year 3.

JFM wishes to obtain short-term monthly forecasts of demand for its products with either simple exponential smoothing or with trend-adjusted exponential smoothing. These simple methods of forecasting are of interest to JFM since forecasts are required for thousands of different items, and since extreme precision is typically not expected in the forecasts. The question that naturally arises is, "Which exponential smoothing model should be used, and what smoothing parameters should be used with it?" As a

EXHIBIT 3.1
Monthly Sales for a Selected Product in JFM Stores

Month	Year 1	Year 2	Year 3
January	17,771	17,134	20,230
February	15,501	15,717	18,441
March	16,619	17,517	19,000
April	12,443	13,510	15,951
May	11,345	10,891	13,881
June	9,901	11,323	12,751
July	8,877	10,656	10,981
August	10,648	11,765	12,981
September	12,652	14,550	17,161
October	14,473	16,890	18,951
November	15,245	17,611	20,191
December	21,468	24,000	29,781

start, we wish to consider how each of these forecasting techniques would have performed on the historical data for the particular product in question.

As a first step, we want to develop a forecast for January of Year 4 with a simple exponential smoothing model, using the value of α that most accurately fits the time series data for this product. The tracking signal values that would have been obtained for each month, as forecasts were being sequentially created with this model, should also be analyzed to consider how consistently the simple exponential smoothing model performs at predicting demand for this particular product. The second stage of the process should develop a forecast for January of Year 4 with a trend-adjusted exponential smoothing model, using the α and δ that most accurately fit the time series data for this particular product. The tracking signal values that would have been obtained for each month, as forecasts were being sequentially created with this model, should be analyzed to consider how consistently this trend-adjusted exponential smoothing model performs while predicting demand for the product in question. Any general observations regarding the efficacy of these forecasting techniques, based on observations from tracking signals, will be of value.

The management of JFM wants the forecasting analysis that is based on this historical data to be conducted in the same fashion that forecasting will be conducted in the future. Since seasonality is a significant issue, seasonal indexes will be updated at the end of every year in order to modify current indexes for possible small changes in seasonal peaks. In keeping with this idea, no forecasting could have been done during the first year of our observations, since trend, seasonality, or random effects could have accounted for any observed monthly changes, and there would have been no way to determine which factors were actually causing these changes.

At the end of the first year, seasonal indexes could have been obtained for use in forecasting during the second year. At the end of the second year, the monthly demands from the first two years could then be combined to obtain forecasts for use in the third year, and so on. Seasonality must be accounted for, but for the sake of simplicity, we shall only consider seasonal indexes that are based on cumulative proportions of monthly sales. Update indexes at the end of each year for use during the following year throughout the analysis.

The data from the first year will be used to get seasonal indexes that can be used in the second year, but no real forecasts will actually be obtained for any month during the first year. Knowledge of these indexes is essential to the analysis; since neither simple exponential smoothing nor trend-adjusted exponential smoothing should be used on demand data that has not been deseasonalized. The data from the first year can be used to establish initial deseasonalized demand values that can be used by both forecasting models that are under consideration.

The first month for which a real forecast should be obtained is January of Year 2. When using a simple exponential smoothing model, some initial deseasonalized forecast from the previous month is required. Start out by estimating the "forecast" for December of Year 1 with the average deseasonalized monthly demand for the first year. This same procedure should be used for the base forecast with trend-adjusted smoothing. Obtaining an initial estimate for the deseasonalized forecast trend component with trend-adjusted smoothing can be more difficult, because we simply do not know what is causing the monthly changes in demand during the first year. For simplicity, we assume that all monthly changes in Year 1 were due to seasonality and random variation, so the deseasonalized trend component for forecasting should be assumed to be zero for December of Year 1, when developing the first real forecast for January of Year 2.

We are ultimately interested in the accuracy of the forecasts that we will actually be using, compared to the actual monthly demand. As a result, MAD values and tracking signals should be computed only for real seasonalized forecasts, not on deseasonalized forecasts, starting in January of Year 2. They should also be based only upon information that is available up to the month in which the forecast is being made. That is, in any given month, we will know the forecasts that we have had up through that given month, and we will know the monthly demand that was actually observed up through that given month. However, we will not know what is going to happen in any months that follow that given month.

The management of JFM has also raised an additional issue that is related to the general notion of the typical measurement of "accuracy" of forecasting methods. It turns out in reality that very different costs are incurred when you overforecast demand, rather than underforecast demand. If you overforecast, the forecasted demand is greater than the actual demand, and you incur extra costs from purchasing and holding too much inventory. If you underforecast, the forecasted demand is less than the actual demand, and you will suffer from stockouts and you will then have some unhappy customers as a result. This is a very critical issue in this particular situation, since JFM has a very loyal customer base and the management is extremely sensitive to promoting customer satisfaction.

It would be difficult to attach specific dollar amounts to the costs for these types of forecast errors. However, a rough subjective assessment by JFM management concludes that the unit cost of underforecasting should be considered to be about four times more than the unit cost of overforecasting demand. JFM wants some insight as to how much the α and δ of the trend-adjusted exponential smoothing model that "most accurately" fits the time series for this particular product would be altered, along with the associated forecast for January of Year 4, when this "cost perspective" of forecasting error is considered.*

---

*__Technical note:__ If you use the "Solver" option in Excel to search for the specific α and δ that minimize MAD, be careful to use multiple starting points in the α and δ cells at the start of the search to avoid the possibility of obtaining "local minimum" solutions for MAD.

Sanderson Produce Co.

Sanderson Produce Co. (SPC) is a large firm that is a wholesale supplier for fruits and vegetables in North Dakota. The firm obtains products from numerous international sources, and it can therefore easily supply most produce on nearly a year-round basis. SPC obtains advance contracts from suppliers to deliver this produce, and the firm has experienced an increase in its market share over the past several years. This increase has been primarily due to SPC's ability to deliver good-quality products to customers in a timely fashion. The firm is committed to continuing this effort, and SPC would find it very useful to have reasonably accurate forecasts of quarterly demand for its products in order to give some advance notice of anticipated demand and of the resulting contracts that must be filled. This advance notice is very useful during preliminary contract negotiations with potential suppliers. SPC management is only interested in short-term forecasts for this application, and they also realize that it is not reasonable to expect to obtain extremely precise forecasts for products of this type.

The problem of obtaining forecasts of demand for produce is made more difficult as a result of seasonality that exists in the demand patterns for some items. As an example of these seasonal effects, the quarterly demand for oranges for the past five years is given in Exhibit 4.1, where demand values are given in terms of standard shipping units that are common for the produce industry. This data represents 20 consecutive quarters of observations, starting in Q1 of Year 1 and ending with Q4 of Year 5. The seasonal effect in the demand for oranges is primarily due to the tastes of consumers, with demand being highest in winter months and lowest in summer months. Since oranges could be obtained from international sources on nearly a year-round basis, this seasonality is not driven from the supply side.

SPC wishes to develop short-term demand forecasts for each of its many different products with a simple forecasting procedure. As a result, only simple exponential smoothing and trend-adjusted exponential smoothing are being considered for use. The

EXHIBIT 4.1
Quarterly Demand for Oranges at SPC

Quarter	Year 1	Year 2	Year 3	Year 4	Year 5
1	173,200	166,000	181,400	193,600	211,800
2	145,400	147,000	151,800	165,800	175,200
3	82,000	86,000	95,000	106,200	109,800
4	128,200	138,000	141,800	155,000	165,800

question that naturally arises is, "Which of these exponential smoothing models should be used, and what smoothing parameters should be used with these models to obtain the best expected overall accuracy from forecasts?" Some insight to the answer to this question can be attained by using the data set from Exhibit 4.1 as a test case to determine how well the different forecasting techniques would have performed if they had been in use over the given five year interval.

As mentioned above, there is an obvious seasonality that must be accounted for in this case, and neither of these exponential smoothing models should be used directly with data sets that contain seasonal effects. This leads to a need for seasonal indexes. SPC management wants to have a forecasting model that updates seasonal indexes at the end of each given year to account for demand values that were observed during the given year. This will be helpful in dealing with any possible small shifts in the seasonal indexes that might be occurring over time. In order to reflect this idea, our analysis will treat the problem as if data is being rolled out in a sequential fashion over time. That is, we can only use data that would have been observed up to any given quarter in the sequence, with no knowledge of what demand values might have been in any future quarters. In order to keep the forecasting procedure as simple as possible, computation of seasonal indexes should be based on simple proportions of observed quarterly demand values.

As a result of the policy of analyzing data as it is rolled out over time, we can do no real forecasting during Year 1, since the observed changes in quarterly values could have been due to seasonality, trend effects, or random fluctuation. There is no way for us to determine what is causing these observed changes as they occur. However, once the entire first year's demand has been observed, seasonal indexes can be directly computed for use during the second year, which will inherently assume that all observed changes in quarterly demand during Year 1 were due to seasonal effects. At the end of the second calendar year, seasonal indexes can be updated to accumulate observations from the first two years, and these updated indexes can then be used in the third year. You should update indexes at the end of each calendar year, and then use the accumulated results that would have been observed up to that point for forecasts during the following year.

The observed demand from the four quarters of Year 1 can also be used to develop initial deseasonalized forecast estimates that are required to start making forecasts with the exponential smoothing models. The first real forecast will be for Q1 of Year 2, and the use of simple exponential smoothing requires an estimated deseasonalized forecast from Q4 of Year 1 to use as a starting point. The estimated deseasonalized "forecast" for Q4 of Year 1 should be obtained as the average deseasonalized quarterly demand from Year 1. This estimate can also be used as the starting base forecast component for Q4 of Year 1 for trend-adjusted exponential smoothing. The initial deseasonalized trend component estimate for Q4 of Year 1 should be assumed to be zero.

The overall accuracy of the forecasting models that are being considered should be based on mean absolute deviation (MAD), using the differences between seasonalized quarterly forecasts and their associated actual observed demands. The MAD values should only be calculated for the relevant quarters when real forecasts were being generated, starting with Q1 of Year 2. We want to develop a forecast for Q1 of Year 6 with simple exponential smoothing, using the α value that most accurately fits the trial data set. The tracking signal values that would have been obtained for each quarter should also be computed, with MAD values and tracking signals being calculated as the quarterly demand values are sequentially rolled out. We also want to develop a forecast for Q1 of Year 6 with trend-adjusted exponential smoothing, using the values of α and δ that most accurately fit the trial data set with trend adjusted exponential smoothing. Tracking-signal values should also be calculated for each quarter, as they were for the simple exponential smoothing forecasts. Any observations regarding the efficacy of using these forecasting techniques on the demand data from this particular example, based on observations from the computed tracking signals, will be of interest to the management of SPC.

The management of SPC has also raised some additional issues regarding the forecasting techniques that might be used. In reality, very different costs are incurred, depending upon whether you overforecast demand or underforecast demand. If you overforecast actual demand for any quarter, you will be contracting to buy more produce than will be required. Some types of surplus produce will have to be discarded as a complete loss, while other types of produce can be sold at a discount. Some types can be sold only at significant discount, to be used as food for animals. Other types of produce can be sold to canneries for a less significant discount. If you underforecast, you will not be able to meet demand, which will result in lost sales, and you will also have some unhappy customers as a result. Such an outcome would be in sharp contrast with the company's commitment to meeting the needs of customers, as discussed above. However, the high cost of routinely discarding or discounting surplus produce would be prohibitive for SPC to absorb on a long-term basis.

Given all of this information, the use of the standard measures of "accuracy" of overall forecast error might be called into question. The SPC management estimates that the penalty cost for overforecasting should be assessed as roughly six times as much per unit of forecast error as the penalty cost for underforecasting. They are interested in having some insight on the significance of the impact that this relative cost consideration might have on standard forecasting techniques, relative to the results that were found above. This impact can be shown by developing a quarterly forecast for Q1 of Year 6, with the same exponential smoothing forecasting model that was considered to be most accurate in the first part of this study. However, the parameters for the "most accurate" forecasting model in this situation should be determined on the basis of trying to minimize the total overall cost of forecasting error.*

---

*Technical note:** If you use the "Solver" option in Excel to search for the specific α and δ that minimize MAD, be careful to use multiple starting points in the α and δ cells at the start of the search to avoid the possibility of obtaining "local minimum" solutions for MAD.

Easton Paper Container Co.

Easton Paper Container Company (EPC) is a medium-sized company in the Mid-Atlantic States that produces small folding cardboard containers. EPC supplies many different types of these boxes to many different types of customers, including food processors and pharmaceutical companies. One of the primary product lines for the business comes from supplying candy companies with small multi-colored boxes. There is very little difference in the way that any of these boxes are produced by EPC, with the exception of the printing process, which varies with the number of different colors that are used in the exterior design. Boxes are primarily distinguished by their size. The X-Series Box is a frequently used size for candy containers, and it is a major product line for EPC.

Variation in the demand for X-Series Boxes stems from several factors, but the major component is due to seasonal variation in the demand for candy. The major peak in demand for candy is based upon Halloween sales. This holiday has a significant impact on box orders in September and October. Forecasting for this particular product line is also made more difficult since the manager believes that the seasonal variation in demand has been shifting over time, reflecting changes in the relative impact of Halloween-driven sales, compared to the sales for other holidays. Exhibit 5.1 shows monthly demand for X-Series Boxes over the past seven years. This data represents 84 consecutive months of historical demand values, starting in January of Year 1 and ending in December of Year 7. These monthly demand values are given in terms of the number of shipping units. There is also an obvious generally increasing trend component in the monthly demand for these boxes when we look at the demand for any particular month over the seven years of observations.

EPC wishes to evaluate some different simple forecasting techniques to obtain reasonably accurate short-term predictions of monthly demand for each of its many different product lines. We will do this by using the data for the demand of X-Series Boxes as a test case for comparing different forecasting models, since the monthly demand for other types of boxes is similar in nature to the demand for X-Series Boxes. Obviously, the demand for boxes for other types of products would have very different seasonal patterns, depending upon the specific product in question. However, the same general types of cyclic patterns prevail for all product lines. This data set will also be a

EXHIBIT 5.1 **Monthly Demand for X-Series Boxes at EPC**

Month	Year 1	2	3	4	5	6	7
January	38,971	40,456	43,589	48,413	55,104	52,802	54,405
February	47,616	54,287	55,797	59,085	65,475	64,124	71,504
March	51,919	59,503	61,319	63,226	69,446	71,739	78,975
April	73,124	77,231	91,543	89,618	102,892	106,386	109,070
May	43,121	48,103	50,190	58,112	59,762	62,878	73,537
June	38,120	42,444	44,900	51,002	58,572	63,823	68,129
July	36,190	40,451	46,655	54,728	63,124	58,668	65,152
August	45,192	53,983	55,992	63,686	75,542	81,322	91,209
September	72,431	87,956	92,985	109,213	122,399	135,263	155,614
October	81,209	91,432	108,515	121,098	141,241	146,440	177,816
November	34,901	40,893	49,135	62,319	74,652	84,512	103,127
December	58,129	65,432	66,218	78,654	101,987	104,717	121,309

good test case since the apparent existence of a significant trend component adds an additional dimension to the complexity of forecasting. As a first step, we wish to evaluate some basic forecasting techniques on the basis of standard measures of forecast accuracy.

Simple exponential smoothing and trend-adjusted exponential smoothing will be the two forecasting models that we will consider for use. Neither of these two models should be used directly on data that contains seasonality, so there is an obvious need to obtain seasonal indexes for each month. Since we want to focus on simple models that give reasonable accuracy forecasts, seasonal indexes should be computed on the basis of simple monthly proportions of observed demand. But, there is an additional problem, given the concern that there is some significant shifting in these seasonal indexes, as discussed above. We will address this issue by using a procedure to compute seasonal indexes that will make the indexes much more reactive to any recent shifts in demand patterns.

To do this, the seasonal indexes will be discarded at the end of each given calendar year, and new indexes will be computed based solely on the data that was observed during the given year in question. As a result, no forecasts can be obtained during the first year since the changes that are observed in monthly demand could have resulted from seasonal effects, trend effects, or random fluctuations. However, we can obtain monthly indexes from the demand that was observed in the first year and then use them during the second year. At the end of the second calendar year, new indexes will be obtained, based solely on the observations in that year, to continue forecasting during the third year, and so on, for each successive year.

Both exponential smoothing models also require some initial deseasonalized forecast estimates before any deseasonalized forecasts can be obtained. The simple exponential smoothing model can be used to make the first deseasonalized forecast for January of Year 2 based on an initial deseasonalized forecast estimate for December of Year 1, which should be the average deseasonalized demand from Year 1. As a result of this, the deseasonalized monthly forecast for January of Year 2 will be the same as the deseasonalized demand in December of Year 1.

The average overall accuracy of any forecasting technique will be based on the mean absolute deviation (MAD) that is obtained from the trial data set, when using that forecasting technique. EPC management is only going to be concerned about the accuracy of the final seasonalized forecasts, so deviations should be based on differences in seasonalized forecasts and actual observed monthly demand, starting with the January forecast in Year 2. Tracking signal values should also be obtained for each month, given only the information that would have been available up through that particular month.

Trend-adjusted smoothing requires both an initial estimate of a base forecast amount and an estimate of the initial trend component for demand. The initial seasonal indexes are being computed from the Year 1 data, assuming that all variation in the first year was due to seasonality alone. In order to obtain initial forecast estimates for trend adjusted smoothing in December of Year 1, we must use some additional information from the observation for January of Year 2. The initial deseasonalized trend component for December of Year 1 should be obtained as the difference between the deseasonalized observed demands for January of Year 2 and December of Year 1. The initial estimated base forecast for December of Year 1 should then be backed out of the data so that that the total deseasonalized forecast for December of Year 1 will be equal to its deseasonalized observed value. This will make the final seasonalized forecasts for both December of Year 1 and January of Year 2 identical to their actual observed demand. MAD values and tracking signals should be computed as they were for simple exponential smoothing, but they should be based on real forecasts, which start with February of Year 2 for trend-adjusted smoothing.

There is significant interest in determining which forecasting technique tends to perform the best at being the most accurate on the test data set. We want to develop a forecast for January of Year 8 with simple exponential smoothing, using the value of α that fits the data most accurately. Then we want to develop a forecast for January of Year 8 with trend-adjusted exponential smoothing using the values of α and δ that fit the data most accurately. Any observations that can be drawn from examining the tracking signals associated with these particular results would be very helpful in the determination of which forecasting technique tends to be performing the best on an overall basis.

Obtaining reasonable short-term forecasts for monthly demand for each of the many different types of boxes is an important issue for EPC, and EPC management realizes that forecasts for each specific product line cannot be perfect. Once short-term forecasts are obtained, monthly schedules are set to produce the different types of boxes. When a forecast turns out to be different than actual demand, EPC sustains incremental costs that are directly related to the magnitude of the forecast error. If we overforecast, so that the monthly forecast is greater than the actual observed monthly demand, the major contribution to the incremental cost comes from the added storage cost for holding excess output for future use. Some incremental cost is also incurred in this situation of overforecasting as a result of having to reschedule workers to other jobs if it is necessary to cut back on the scheduled output from some of the lines of boxes. If the overestimate of demand is excessive or if it goes on for too long, it may be necessary to suddenly place some workers on temporary layoff.

If we underforecast, with monthly forecasts being lower than the actual observed monthly demand, the primary incremental cost will be incurred from the potential loss of sales and from a loss of goodwill with EPC's customers. An overtime premium must also be paid if workers are called on to work extra hours to cover the difference between scheduled and actual requirements. If the underestimate of demand is excessive or if it goes on for too long, it might be necessary to incur substantial start-up costs for temporary extra shifts.

Given all of this information about having different costs for overforecasting and underforecasting, the use of MAD as the standard for measuring forecast accuracy might be called into question. It would indeed be very difficult to obtain any precise estimates of these associated costs for forecasting error. However, the EPC manager has given us a rough subjective estimate that the relative penalty cost for underforecasting monthly demand should be assessed as three times as much per unit of forecast error as the penalty cost for overforecasting monthly demand. It is of definite interest to determine the impact that this relative-cost consideration might have on the forecasting techniques that were selected above, when MAD was used as the standard for accuracy in our initial analysis.

To make this determination, it will be sufficient to re-do the analysis above for trend-adjusted smoothing to find the values of α and δ that will minimize the total cost of forecasting error on the trial data set, rather than minimizing MAD. It is of particular interest to know how much the forecast for January of Year 8 will change when a forecasting model is used to minimize this total cost of forecast error.*

---

*Technical note: If you use the "Solver" option in Excel to search for the specific α and δ that minimize MAD, be careful to use multiple starting points in the α and δ cells at the start of the search, to avoid the possibility of obtaining "local minimum" solutions for MAD.

Waiting Lines

James-Younger Trust Co.

James-Younger Trust Co. (JYT) is an old established family-owned regional bank with a number of branches throughout the midwestern states. The majority of JYT branches are in Missouri, but offices exist in other states, including Minnesota and Alabama. JYT management wants to examine policies for staffing tellers in branch banks, as a result of having received some negative feedback regarding excessive times for waiting in lines from a customer survey conducted by the bank's customer service department. This negative feedback could be a legitimate concern, or it could be resulting from the common phenomenon that customers typically feel that they are waiting longer than they actually are waiting. If this latter phenomenon is the case, then additional staffing might not be the most effective solution to resolving the problem.

The operation at the branch bank in Dillinger, Missouri, has been monitored over a prolonged period to get some idea of the patterns of customer arrivals and service times. JYT management wants to use this data to analyze the expected impact that changes in teller staffing would have on some standard measures of customer service. More specifically, they want to know what impact increased teller staffing would have on the time that an average customer would be expected to take for the combined time of waiting in line and having a teller perform their transaction. It is also of interest to know what the impact of additional staffing would be on the average number of customers who are waiting in the system, either in line or being serviced. JYT management is willing to absorb the incremental expense of staffing additional tellers if the amount of time that customers are waiting in the system does indeed seem to be unacceptable with their current staffing policies.

Sample observations regarding customer arrival patterns at the Dillinger branch were taken by counting the number of customers who arrived at the branch during one-minute intervals. Customer arrival patterns vary significantly during different time intervals each day and they also vary over different days of the week. The specific time interval that was chosen for study in this particular analysis was for the peak period of customer demand, between 11:30 A.M. and 1:30 P.M. on Fridays. Arrival patterns are consistent during this time interval. A bank employee was used to monitor the number of arrivals at the branch during randomly selected one-minute time intervals over a number of different Fridays, between 11:30 A.M. and 1:30 P.M. The results of these

EXHIBIT 6.1
Arrival Patterns for Customers at the Dillinger Branch of JYT

Arrivals per One-Minute Interval	Frequency
0	20
1	54
2	202
3	266
4	431
5	539
6	531
7	514
8	389
9	217
10	77
11	53
12	45
13	20
14	17
15	16
16	10
17	6
18	2

observations for arrivals per one-minute interval are given in Exhibit 6.1. We see, for example, that there were 202 different one-minute intervals during which exactly two customers arrived at the branch office during the sampling procedure.

When customers come into the Dillinger branch for service, they enter a cordoned system in which they wait in a single-file line. Once they reach the front of the waiting line, they then go to the first available teller to complete their transaction. Each of the customers who entered during the period of random sampling that resulted in the arrival pattern for Exhibit 6.1 was also observed to determine the amount of time that it took for a teller to process their transaction. This time measurement for having the service performed did not include any time during which the customer had waited in line.

Most of the observed service times were quite short since many of the customers were performing very simple transactions. A typical transaction would consist of a customer making a loan payment from a coupon payment book, or a customer making a simple deposit to a checking account while using deposit slips from their check registers. The transactions could not be observed too precisely in order to avoid the possibility of disturbing both customers and tellers. As a result, times were recorded only in 15-second time intervals, and the results are summarized in Exhibit 6.2, in units of minutes required for the completion of transactions. We see from Exhibit 6.2 that 6,642 customers had their transactions completed in some time that ranged between .2500 minutes (15 seconds) and .4999 minutes (30 seconds).

The quality assurance manager at JYT is quite certain that the sampling results that are summarized in Exhibits 6.1 and 6.2 are reasonably accurate since the observations were quite easy to measure. Moreover, the observed results fit with the JYT manager's general perception of patterns of arrival rates and service times during the peak demand period that has been specified.

The queuing models that must be used to obtain the expected times that we are seeking will be making some assumptions about the specific types of probability distributions that describe the data for arrival patterns and service times. Before performing any such analysis, you will have to verify that these assumptions are valid for this particular application. The expected number of arrivals per one-minute time interval, λ, can be computed from the sample data set. The probability for various numbers of arrivals per one-minute interval can then be computed with the assumption that the arrival pattern follows a Poisson distribution, using the computed λ. An easy way to determine whether or not the assumption of a Poisson probability distribution for arrival patterns is valid can be checked by simultaneously plotting the observed distribution of probabilities for

EXHIBIT 6.2
Service Time (in Minutes) for Customers at the Dillinger Branch of JYT

Interval Start Time	Interval Finish Time	Frequency
0.0000	0.2499	9,949
0.2500	0.4999	6,642
0.5000	0.7499	2,401
0.7500	0.9999	700
1.0000	1.2499	508
1.2500	1.4999	120
1.5000	1.7499	78
1.7500	1.9999	39
2.0000	2.2499	13
2.2500	2.4999	3

the number of arrivals in one-minute intervals with the associated probabilities with the assumed Poisson distribution. The plots of the two distributions should look similar.

The situation is a bit more complicated when considering the distribution of service times because that data is reported in terms of time intervals for service times. We can see that 9,949 customers had their transactions completed in a time that ranged between 0.0000 and 0.2499 minutes, but we do not know the precise time that any customer took for service. We can assume that all customers had their service completed in the time that is at the midpoint for the time interval in which their service time is reported, in order to calculate the expected service time for the distribution. This can then be used to get the expected service rate, μ. We can then determine the expected probability that the time for service takes t or longer as $e^{-\mu t}$, with the assumption that service time patterns fit a negative exponential distribution. We can then simultaneously plot these expected probabilities with the associated probabilities from the observed distribution. In doing this, the plot should be done for t values that are at the starting points for intervals. We used the midpoint values of the intervals for arithmetic simplicity to obtain the expected completion time, but that assumption is not valid when we are considering the probability that service times take a time t or longer for completion. However, all observations in an interval must obviously take longer than the start time of that interval for completion.

Once we have verified that the distribution assumptions are valid, appropriate queuing models can then be used to obtain the desired expected measures of customer service. The JYT manager specifically wants to know the impact that increased teller staffing would have on the expected number of customers in the system and on the expected customer waiting time in the system. It is possible to staff up to six tellers, given the existing configuration of the Dillinger branch. The manager's questions can be answered simply by seeing a summary chart. That chart should show the expected time that a customer spends in the system, and the expected number of customers that are in the system for each of the possible different staffing options that allow for as many as six tellers to be staffed at the Dillinger branch. The incremental benefit of staffing additional tellers can then be determined from the summary chart.

Scott's Processing Systems

Scott's Processing Systems (SPS) is a business that is highly dependent upon the proper functioning of a large number of similar pieces of equipment that are subject to periodic breakdown. A problem currently facing SPS is the proper staffing of equipment maintenance workers in order to minimize expected total cost. The expected total cost that is associated with this decision has two primary components. These include the cost of compensation for employing the maintenance repair workers and the incremental expected downtime cost that is incurred while equipment is not operating. The downtime cost primarily results from lost wages that must be paid to workers who are idle when workstations are not operating, since extra hours must accordingly be built into the schedule for the facility to meet its required output levels. This issue is particularly a problem if the extra hours result in overtime operation to make up for the lost downtime.

Maintenance workers who repair the machines each receive a total compensation of $37.50 per hour. Due to the nature of the repair work, there is no benefit to having the maintenance workers operate together as a team, so each worker goes out on repair jobs on an individual basis as repair calls are received. As a result, more than one repair call can be performed simultaneously, with one mechanic working at each repair location. Repairs are performed on inoperative machines at the breakdown location. The machines are highly profitable work centers, and the cost of having one of them inoperable is $450 per hour for each machine that is not operating. Machines remain inoperable during the time that maintenance workers are repairing them, so downtime cost is incurred during the entire time that each machine is down. Maintenance workers are dispatched to repair machines on a first come–first served basis, as the calls for service are received.

Records have been evaluated for the previous six months of operation at SPS, during a total of 1,044 hours of operation at the facility, to obtain some information on breakdown rates for these machines and the associated times for repairing them. The number of reported breakdowns that occurred during one-hour time periods was found to range between 0 and 9. Exhibit 7.1 shows the summary data from the maintenance records, to show the distribution of the number of breakdowns per hour. For example, there were 217 different one-hour intervals during which there were exactly three breakdowns.

EXHIBIT 7.1
Distribution of Hourly Breakdowns at SPS

Breakdowns per Hour	Frequency
0	95
1	198
2	277
3	217
4	149
5	60
6	35
7	6
8	6
9	1

The same maintenance records that led to the results in Exhibit 7.1 were also evaluated to determine the associated repair time that it took for each of the 2,608 total breakdowns that occurred during that time period. These times include the travel time that it took for workers to get to the machines. Due to the nature of the way in which worker times for repairs have been reported, we only know that repair times for machines fall within some given time intervals of 0.2-hour (12-minute) duration. Repair times never exceeded a value of 2.4 hours for completion, and the reported repair times had the frequencies that are shown in Exhibit 7.2. For example, there were 242 breakdowns that took between .400 hr. (24 minutes) and .599 hr. (36 minutes) to have repairs completed. However, the exact completion time is not known for any of the repairs.

The previous six months were quite normal at SPS, in terms of both the operation of the equipment and the performance of the workers, so the values that are reported in Exhibit 7.2 can be considered representative of normal operating conditions for the facility. As a first step, we are interested in determining the number of maintenance workers that should be staffed to minimize the expected total cost per hour for maintaining the equipment. This expected cost should include both the hourly compensation for employees and the expected hourly cost for equipment downtime. This is clearly going to require the use of some waiting line models.

Before any waiting line models can be employed, it will be necessary to verify that all underlying assumptions used by these models are valid in this case. The primary assumptions of interest relate to the probability models that are used to describe the distributions of both breakdown patterns and service times.

Breakdown patterns are typically assumed to follow a Poisson distribution with waiting line models. This assumption can be verified by examining the data set from Exhibit 7.1, in comparison to the outcomes that would be expected if that data set actually does have a Poisson distribution.

EXHIBIT 7.2
Distribution of Repair Times (in Hours) at SPS

Interval Start	Interval End	Interval Frequency
0.000	0.199	1,252
0.200	0.399	582
0.400	0.599	242
0.600	0.799	172
0.800	0.999	157
1.000	1.199	110
1.200	1.399	40
1.400	1.599	17
1.600	1.799	15
1.800	1.999	12
2.000	2.199	6
2.200	2.399	3

The information in Exhibit 7.1 can be used to determine the observed probabilities that various numbers of breakdowns per hour actually occurred. The associated expected number of breakdowns per hour, λ, can then be derived. The Poisson probabilities for the number of breakdowns per hour can then be calculated, with a mean value of λ for the distribution. The simultaneous plotting of the observed probabilities and the theoretical probabilities for number of breakdowns per hour should appear to be very similar in nature.

Repair times that come from a random probability distribution for completion are typically assumed to have a negative exponential distribution. The data set in Exhibit 7.2 can be used to obtain the probabilities that repair times fall within the given time intervals. Since nothing is known about the precise completion time for the repair of any particular breakdown, we will assume that every repair time in a given interval was completed at exactly the midpoint time of the given interval. This certainly did not really happen, but it is a reasonable assumption to make when we simply want to compute the expected completion time for a repair. The value of the expected service rate, μ, can then be calculated directly from the expected service time.

The assumption that service times fit a negative exponential distribution can be evaluated easily by considering the cumulative probability that the time for a given service repair takes a time t, or longer, for completion. These cumulative probabilities can be obtained from Exhibit 7.2 for t values that represent the start times for the intervals. Obviously, this probability is 1.000 when we have $t = 0.000$. It is not reasonable to assume that all observed times are at the interval midpoint for these particular computations. However, we do know that all observations within an interval fall above the start time for that particular interval. If this distribution is negative exponential, then the theoretical values for these cumulative probabilities are given by $e^{-\mu t}$. The simultaneous plotting of these observed and theoretical cumulative probabilities should display very similar characteristics.

Once the assumptions about the distributions for breakdowns and service times have been verified, it is possible to start considering the expected cost values that are of primary interest to the SPS manager. In particular, we can staff up to four maintenance workers to do repairs, given the current configuration of things at SPS. Maintenance workers can perform no other tasks during time periods when they are not actively repairing equipment, since this would interfere with their ability to respond quickly to repair calls. Each maintenance worker will receive their total hourly compensation, whether they are working at repairing equipment, or are just waiting for repair calls. The SPS manager wants to know the total expected hourly cost that corresponds to each feasible staffing option, using up to a maximum of four maintenance workers.

THE POTENTIAL IMPACT OF NEW TECHNOLOGY

A second issue is also a major concern to the manager of SPS. This issue is related to the availability of some new technology that would significantly alter the way in which equipment repair is currently being performed at SPS. As we might have expected, the cost of modifying the existing facility to accommodate the implementation of this new technology would be a very expensive option, so the manager is seeking some input regarding the expected payoff value from its adoption. This new technology would allow SPS to significantly reduce the time that is needed to make machines operational after a breakdown. This option sounds particularly appealing when the high cost of equipment downtime is considered, but the initial expense for implementing the option is very high.

With this new system SPS would staff the same number of mechanics that were found to minimize the total cost for the existing system, but they would perform the repairs in a very different manner. One of the maintenance workers would take a shuttle cart to any machine that was in need of repair, and replace the appropriate equipment module within the inoperable machine to get it back on line at a relatively short period of time. With these modules, the maintenance worker would not actually be repairing any equipment components on location, but would simply be removing a defective module from the equipment and plugging a functioning module in its place. The idea here is similar to the logic used when replacing an entire circuit board in a piece of electronic equipment to get it operating quickly, rather than taking the time to try to find and replace the specific defective component on the board while the equipment is not working. The shuttle cart would always carry a variety of different repair modules, to be prepared to deal with any breakdown. This same maintenance worker would then return the defective equipment module to a central processing center where it would be scheduled for repair, and then take a rebuilt module from storage to put onto the cart to replace the one that was just used.

Since the replacement of these modules is nearly an automatic process, the worker would be able to get machines operating with a fixed service time of approximately 10 minutes, including travel time to get to the machines. The plan is to have one maintenance worker being used to replace modules, to efficiently get inoperative machines back on line, while the other maintenance workers would specialize in repairing the defective modules that had been brought back to the central processing center. Due to the substantial capital expense for the equipment needed to set up a mechanic to replace modules at inoperative machines, it is not considered economically feasible to have equipment for more than one worker to perform this module replacement function at the same time. The maintenance worker who makes the machines operational and retrieves the modules will also repair defective modules at the central processing center when there are no calls to repair machines. It can be assumed that the equipment breakdown rates, shown in Exhibit 7.1, will remain the same with the module replacement system as they have been with the existing system.

SPS will still need to staff mechanics so that there are sufficient labor hours available to repair all of the modules after they have been taken back to the central processing center. It is expected that the process of repairing modules at the central processing center should be able to be done much more efficiently than in the existing situation, since the module repair workers will not have the natural distractions that arise when they are trying to repair equipment on location in the operating facility. Since the central processing facility would be dedicated exclusively to performing repairs on modules, it can be set up for more efficient operation. There would also be a reduced likelihood of events such as having maintenance workers going back to retrieve tools that had been left behind at the location of the previous repair job.

Given all of this, the average time to repair modules at the central processing facility would be expected to be significantly less, on average, than the average time that it currently takes to repair machines on location. The time that would be saved by this feature is expected to be more than adequate to compensate for the additional labor time that it would take for the worker to perform the module replacement operation. Therefore, we assume that this new system can operate effectively with the same total number of maintenance workers that we chose to minimize expected total cost under the existing scenario.

Since the cost for converting the existing system to allow for the implementation of the new technology is quite expensive, we are interested in knowing the expected savings in total operating cost per hour that would result if the new technology were to be implemented. The SPS manager also wants to start gathering any other information that we will need to make a final decision about the overall benefit of acquiring the new technology. Any additional preliminary insight that can be given about the information that we will ultimately require to adequately address the issue would be very helpful in giving the SPS manager some advance notice to begin the job of gathering the necessary information.*

---

*Technical note: Linear interpolation should be used to obtain any values from waiting line tables.

Polonius National Bank

Polonius National Bank (PNB) is a large regional bank with many branches in the Pacific Northwest. Most of these branch banks are located in relatively small hamlets in the region, but some of the branch offices are located in larger cities. The customer service manager at PNB is concerned about some negative feedback that has been reported both in customer surveys and in a limited number of written complaints from customers. Most of these complaints have centered on the possibility that customers are spending unacceptable amounts of time in waiting times at some PNB branches. There are some benchmark standards that PNB uses for measuring the level of acceptability of such customer service characteristics. As a result of all of this, the manager wants to examine the existing policies for staffing cashiers in PNB branch banks.

As a first step, some information has been gathered regarding patterns of waiting line activity in PNB branches. The operation at the branch bank in Bard, Oregon, was monitored to get some idea of both the patterns for customer arrivals at the facility and of the distribution of transaction completion times. There are obviously different arrival rate patterns at banks during different times of the day, on different days of the week, and on some specific days of the month. A decision was made to select one particular time frame during which the arrival patterns and service time patterns at the branch could be expected to be consistent. Sample observations regarding customer arrival patterns at the branch were taken by counting the number of customers who arrived during one-minute intervals. All of the observations were made at randomly selected times between 9:00 A.M. and 11:30 A.M. over a number of different days. The expected number of arrivals per minute tends to be greater during the time interval 11:30 A.M. to 1:00 P.M., when customers make banking transactions over their lunch hour. Different staffing policies would obviously be called for during these different situations, so observations were stopped at 11:30 A.M. in order to have a consistent period of observations. Staffing policies for time periods other than the interval between 9:00 A.M. and 11:30 A.M. can be considered later, once this initial analysis has been completed.

A particularly conscientious branch employee was given the task of counting customers as they arrived at the branch and recording the results. The results of the observations are summarized in Exhibit 8.1, where it shows, for example, that there were 26 of the observed one-minute intervals during which exactly one customer arrived at the bank.

EXHIBIT 8.1
Summary
Data for
Observations
of Customer
Arrivals
at PNB

Customer Arrivals per Minute	Frequency
0	11
1	26
2	101
3	123
4	207
5	225
6	188
7	166
8	90
9	55
10	32
11	16
12	12
13	8
14	4
15	3
16	3
17	2
18	1

The manager also has easy access to the total number of transactions that took place during these 9:00 A.M. to 11:30 A.M. time slots, and the arrival results in Exhibit 8.1 are generally consistent with that information. The data was relatively easy to measure, and we also have this independent support for the notion that everything was measured properly, so the customer arrival data can be accepted as being valid.

Each of the customers who entered the PNB branch bank during this sampling event was also observed to determine the amount of time that it took for their transaction to be processed by a teller. The transaction time that was measured did not include any of the time that customers stood in line while waiting for the next available teller to complete their transaction. Following the direction of many high-traffic walk-in service facilities and most banks, PNB uses a cordoned system, which customers walk through to keep service on a first come–first served basis. Most of the observed service times were quite short, since most of them were very simple transactions. A typical transaction would consist of having a customer making a simple deposit to a checking account or making an installment loan payment.

None of these transactions could be observed with great precision, since it was very important to avoid being disruptive to any interactions that took place between the customers and tellers. As a result, each of the transaction times was simply recorded as falling into some given 15-second time interval. The results of all of these observations are summarized in Exhibit 8.2. We can see, for example, that there were a total of 2,159 observed transactions that required between 15 seconds (.250 minutes) and 30 seconds (.499 minutes) for completion.

EXHIBIT 8.2
Summary
Data for
Observations
of Customer
Transaction
Times
(in Minutes)
at PNB

Interval Start Time	Interval Finish Time	Frequency
0.000	0.249	3,683
0.250	0.499	2,159
0.500	0.749	460
0.750	0.999	358
1.000	1.249	140
1.250	1.499	97
1.500	1.749	94
1.750	1.999	3
2.000	2.249	5
2.250	2.499	1

The quality assurance manager has the general perception that these service times seem reasonable for the typical mix of customer transactions that take place at the branch during the particular time interval that is being considered. Therefore, we conclude that these observations can be assumed to be accurate.

Waiting line models can be used to determine the expected values of many different customer service characteristics in situations like the one being considered. These characteristics could be things like the expected waiting time in line for a customer or the expected number of customers waiting in the system. However, it is necessary to determine the validity of any assumptions made with such models before they are used. The primary assumptions in waiting line models are typically concerned with the specific probability distributions used to describe both arrival patterns and service time patterns.

Values for the observed probability that various numbers of customers arrive in a one-minute interval can be obtained from the data in Exhibit 8.1, along with the associated expected arrival rate per minute, λ. Distributions for arrivals are typically assumed to have a Poisson distribution in waiting line models. Given the λ value that is obtained from the data in Exhibit 8.1, the associated theoretical Poisson probabilities can be obtained for various numbers of arrivals per minute. A simultaneous plot of the observed probabilities and the theoretical probabilities should have very similar characteristics if the Poisson assumption is valid.

Service completion times are usually assumed to have a negative exponential distribution in waiting line models, when service times have a random distribution. This distribution describes the probability that it takes a given time, t, to complete a transaction in this case. It is much simpler to consider instead the cumulative probability that it takes time t, or longer, to complete the transaction. For example, there is always probability 1.00 that it takes a time $t = 0$, or longer, for service. The data in Exhibit 8.2 can be used to obtain the expected completion time for a transaction. In obtaining the expected service time, it is reasonable to assume that every transaction that is associated with a given time interval took exactly the interval midpoint time for completion. The expected service rate, μ, can then be calculated. Given the value of μ, the theoretical probability that it takes a time t, or longer, for completing a transaction is $e^{-\mu t}$ if the distribution fits a negative exponential distribution.

When we compute the cumulative probability that it takes time t, or longer, for observed transaction times, it is not reasonable to say that all times are at the midpoints for their associated interval. However, all points in an interval certainly take longer than the start time for the interval. As a result, the observed probabilities can be calculated for t values that correspond to the start times of each interval. The simultaneous plotting of the theoretical probabilities from a negative exponential distribution and the observed probabilities, using all times that represent the start of time intervals, should be very similar if the negative exponential assumption is valid.

Once it has been verified that the basic assumptions for a waiting line model have been met, it is possible to start measuring the expected waiting line characteristics that are of particular interest. The PNB manager is interested in approaching this problem with a total cost based analysis. In particular, there are two costs that are associated with this problem. The one cost that is relatively easy to determine is the hourly cost for staffing the tellers who provide the service. The current configuration of this branch office allows for up to a maximum of six tellers to be staffed at any given time. Based on the total compensation that is paid to tellers and other associated costs, PNB will incur a cost of $25 per hour for each teller that it chooses to staff.

It is somewhat more difficult to arrive at an estimate of the hourly cost of goodwill that should be associated with the time each customer must wait in the system before the service is completed. This includes both the time spent waiting in line and the time it takes to complete the transaction. The PNB manager realizes that it would be very difficult to put a precise value on this hourly cost of goodwill. Some hourly cost in the range of six to eight times the hourly cost of staffing a teller is initially given as a rough subjective estimate. However, we need some precise estimate of hourly cost of goodwill to proceed, so a compromise is made. We start by finding the total combined cost per hour for each feasible staffing option that allows up to six tellers to be staffed, when we assume that the cost of goodwill is $175 per hour for each customer who is in the system. The goal is to determine the staffing option that will minimize the expected combined cost per hour of staffing and goodwill, with this assumed cost of customer goodwill.

To make the analysis more realistic, some sensitivity analysis should then be performed. We keep the same number of tellers in place that was determined to minimize the total cost with the $175-per-hour assumption. Then we determine the range of goodwill cost values for which this staffing option will remain the same. That is, we determine how much the estimated cost of goodwill would have to increase before the decision should be made to staff an additional teller. Also, given the initial staffing decision, we find out how much the estimated cost of goodwill would have to decrease before the decision should be made to staff one less teller. If this range of goodwill cost values gives a good buffer around the $175-per-hour estimate, then we can feel relatively secure in the staffing decision. If the range of goodwill values does not give a sufficient buffer around the $175-per-hour estimate, then more effort will have to be given to getting a better estimate of the hourly cost of goodwill that should be used.

Forest Products Association

Forest Products Association (FPA) is an organization of small logging businesses in northern New England that are facing a common problem. All of these logging businesses are located in the same basic geographic area and they all harvest trees that are sent to different processing facilities to be turned into various products, depending upon the specific type of wood. The forests in the area are a mix of hardwood (oak, maple, birch) and softwood (fir, hemlock, spruce, pine) trees. The hardwood trees are mostly varieties of birch trees that are typically turned into products like wooden dowels and toothpicks at regional processing facilities. If birch trees are big enough, they can also be processed into high-grade lumber at one of the regional sawmills. Subcontractors process the low-quality maple and oak into firewood for local use. Good-quality maple and oak can be sent to one of the regional sawmills to be processed into high-grade lumber if there is demand for it. The prices paid for these kinds of wood vary significantly with the existing demand for the product.

The softwood trees have very different uses than the hardwood trees. Higher-quality spruce and pine trees can be sent to the regional sawmills to be processed into lower-grade lumber for different purposes if there is demand for these raw materials at the sawmills. The large majority of the softwood trees are ultimately sent to one of the very large regional paper mills to be used as pulpwood to be processed into newsprint, which is paper of the quality used for newspapers. Each of the logging companies is typically under contract to deliver set quantities of pulpwood to the individual mills over set time intervals. The mix of trees in the area is such that supplying paper mills with pulpwood constitutes a significant majority of the total business for the logging companies.

All of the timber cutting in the area that is done by the small companies is done on a selective-cutting basis. This selective cutting results partially from some state regulations, but it mostly results from the desires of property owners. The small logging companies do not own the land where they cut trees. They do the cutting under contract with many property owners who own tracts of land that are typically in the range of 100 to 200 acres. The property owners have the cutting done periodically to generate some extra revenue, and because they are required to do so in order to remain in a significantly reduced property tax classification that is known as "tree-growth status." These property owners want to have very selective cutting done to maximize the revenue that is generated, while maintaining the forestlike nature of the property. Substantial timber cutting is also done during the summer on excess property that is associated with a local ski resort that has the same basic interests in forest preservation as the other property owners.

Timber cutters enter the property and selectively cut trees based on the age of the trees, on the condition of the trees, and on the existing demand for particular types of wood. The harvested trees have their limbs removed, and all parts of the tree that are three inches or more in diameter are then dragged out to a landing area. Specialized tractorlike vehicles, called skids, drag the tree components to different stacking areas at the landing, depending on where the components are to be sent for processing. When a sufficient amount of any given category of wood has accumulated in a stack at the landing, a logging truck is called in to remove a load of that wood and take it to the appropriate processing facility. A cranelike device, called a picker, grasps logs from the stacks and loads them onto the back of the truck. The trucks for hauling pulpwood are usually the size of a tractor-trailer, and the trailer consists of a flat bed with sets of large steel forks that are mounted upright to retain the logs that are stacked lengthwise on the bed of the trailer. This loading process keeps the logs consistently oriented on the backs of the trucks so that the logs do not shift during the trip to the mill, which would create an unstable and dangerous load. The pulpwood hauling trucks are of different sizes.

A large parent company owns all of the regional paper mills, and the mills have traditionally paid different prices for pulpwood, depending on how it is delivered. The pulpwood must eventually be chipped into small pieces before the process of making newsprint can begin. The mills have paid a higher price per ton for pulpwood that is already chipped when it is delivered. The large timber companies that deal in greater volumes of timber that is cut from their own property have been willing to incur the expense of setting up portable chipping operations at the cutting sites. The softwood is run through the chippers at the landing, and the chips are blown into the back end of an enclosed trailer. This allows for more efficient transport of the pulpwood to the mills, and for very efficient unloading at the mills. Once trucks are checked in and weighed at the mill, the trailers of chips are simply backed onto a platform to which they are secured. A hydraulic mechanism then lifts the front end on the platform, with the attached truck and trailer on it, until all of the chips slide out of the back end of the trailer into a pit. A bulldozer then pushes the dumped chips onto a huge storage pile. This unloading process is completed very quickly, so there is never any waiting time for trucks to be unloaded when they are delivering pulpwood chips. The portable chipping facilities that allow for this increased efficiency are very expensive, but the larger companies also receive the higher price for delivering pulpwood that is already chipped.

The mills maintain a very large safety-stock inventory of chipped pulpwood in their storage yards because it is difficult to predict when deliveries might be unavoidably halted for some reason. This happens whenever the state forest service temporarily stops all logging operations in forests due to the potential of having fires started during prolonged periods without rain. This also happens during "mud season" in the spring when melting snow and rain creates conditions such that the skids simply can not be operated in the forests without bogging down in mud and damaging the root systems of the remaining trees. The public secondary roads that the trucks use also become quite unstable during mud season and they are posted to prohibit heavy-truck traffic until they dry out later in the spring in order to prevent excessive damage to the roadbeds. All logging operations must stop while the public roads are posted during mud season.

The smaller timber companies simply cannot afford to purchase portable chipping facilities on their own. It is also not feasible for them to enter into a partnership agreement to buy a portable chipping facility for joint use because they are all working at different locations and because each location would have an ongoing need for a chipper. The small logging companies are therefore in a position in which they simply have to deliver pulpwood logs to the mills. They then receive a lower payment per ton of pulpwood since the mill has to incur the expense of chipping the wood before it can be used.

THE PROBLEM

All logging companies have recently been notified by the parent company of the mills that the paper mills will only be accepting pulpwood that has not been chipped before delivery for one more year. After one year, the mills will still be glad to deal with the small logging companies, and will pay them the higher price for the delivery of chipped pulpwood, but the small logging companies must find a way to get the pulpwood chipping performed before delivery. The reasons behind this action come from several sources. The paper mills are under extreme pressure to cut costs due to heavy competition from low-cost imported newsprint. In addition, the regional paper mills were all built around the same time and the chipping operations are nearing the end of their expected useful life. Maintenance and repair costs are expected to increase dramatically if they are not replaced.

Putting in new chipping operations at the mills is viewed by the parent company as incurring a major capital expense in order to provide an expensive service to some of their suppliers. The small logging companies have also been making numerous complaints about the amount of time that their drivers must wait in line while making deliveries of pulpwood logs to the chipping operations at the mills. This is also compounded by the fact that the mills must pay union scale wages, that are very high by local standards, to the operators of any on-site chipping facility, while this relatively low-skill requirement activity is quite unrelated to the process of making newsprint. It is believed that an independent operation would be able to provide this service to the small logging companies in a much more efficient and cost-effective manner.

After recovering from the initial shock of this announcement, some of the owners of the small logging companies called the other company owners together to discuss possible solutions to their newly presented common problem. The result of this initial meeting was that all of these owners have agreed to form the FPA cooperative to deal with this issue. First of all, the FPA members have all come to the conclusion that the mills are dealing in good faith and had no other option than to plan the closing of the chipping operations at the mills, given the known background of the decision and the existing business environment. In particular, there is no perceived threat that the mills only want to deal with the large timber companies as a source of supply for pulpwood.

Members of the FPA cooperative are trying to determine the best way to deal with this situation. They have also realized that this situation could actually be beneficial to them in the long run if they can jointly find an efficient solution to getting their pulp-wood chipped, since the mills will continue to pay the higher rate per ton to receive pulpwood that is already chipped.

THE PROPOSED SOLUTION

Members of FPA have concluded that the only feasible options are to establish their own pulpwood chipping operation or to rely upon some independent contractor to es-tablish such a facility. They are currently evaluating the option of establishing their own chipping operation.

Any new chipping operation would be much like the existing operation that the mill currently runs, and it would use the same basic kinds of chippers. Trucks arrive at a yard office where they are weighed. The driver is given a billing ticket that notes the time of arrival, the particular company that the driver is making the delivery for, and the gross weight of the loaded truck. The chipping operation runs 12 hours per day at the mill. The drivers then take the loaded truck down a short road to one of two partic-ular chipping facilities, based upon which one is perceived to have the shortest waiting line time.

The individual chipping facilities are some distance apart for many safety reasons. For example, parts of logs and foreign objects can fly back out of the chippers as they are being fed into the large, high-speed rotating blades that do the actual chipping. There are many dangers involved with being around such a facility and this danger is compounded if the facilities are close together, and protective safety barriers must be present between adjoining facilities. The amount of noise at these facilities is also very intense. Due to the distance between the facilities and the presence of the safety barri-ers, trucks cannot change lines once they have decided upon which chipping facility to go to for processing.

The trucks wait in line at the selected facility until they are ready to be serviced. The truck pulls up next to a picker that loads the logs onto a conveyor that feeds the logs into the chipper. The supervisor of the given chipping facility enters the starting time for processing on the billing ticket. The picker operator carefully unloads the truck to keep the logs going through the chipper in a nearly continuous flow. However, the rate of flow of the logs through the chipper depends upon the diameter of the logs and on the type of wood that is being processed. Logs from fir trees can be run through the chipper very quickly, while some of the harder species of spruce trees are much more dense and require much more time to process. The amount of processing time also de-pends upon the size of the trailer and on how the logs were stacked onto it. The processed chips will be blown into an enclosed trailer at the proposed chipping opera-tion, and the chipped pulpwood will then be hauled to the mill for all of the FPA tim-ber companies.

Once the processing is done at the chipping facility, the driver takes the truck back to the yard office where the truck is weighed again to get its unloaded weight. The billing ticket is then marked with the departure time, the unloaded truck weight, and the net weight of the delivered pulpwood. A copy of the billing ticket is given to the dri-ver, and the timber companies are paid on the basis of the total net weight of all pulp-wood that their trucks deliver each month.

It was mentioned above that there have been numerous complaints from the owners of the timber companies about the amount of time that their drivers must wait in line before processing begins at the existing chipping operation at the mill. There have been no complaints about how long the actual chipping process takes, once it has been started. Three options have been proposed by FPA members as to how the operating procedures of the existing chipping operation might be modified in their proposed co-operative operation to reduce the waiting time in line for drivers.

Option 1

This option originated from a group of drivers, and it seems like a simple and direct solution to the problem of reducing waiting time. Drivers would go through the delivery process that was described above while delivering pulpwood. However, the logs would quickly be dumped off the trucks near one of the chipper facilities, and the picker operators who feed the chippers would remove logs from the dumped stack of logs, rather than pick the logs directly from the trucks.

Unfortunately, this option creates more problems than it solves. The efficiency of the picker operators at the chipping facilities would be greatly reduced if they must pick logs from a disorganized pile of dumped logs, rather than pick logs that are already consistently oriented on the backs of the delivery trucks. Some procedure would also have to be implemented to efficiently dump the logs off of the delivery trucks, which would then increase operating costs at the chipper facilities. Since the timber companies in the FPA cooperative would also be paying the workers at the chipping facilities under this proposed situation, they would end up as net losers under this option. That is, they would save money from having reduced times for drivers waiting in line, but they would incur a much greater cost from lost efficiency from the workers that they are paying at the chipping operation as a result.

Option 2

Some of the drivers also suggested the basic notion behind this option. The idea is that excessive waiting times at the existing chipping operation at the mill have not been the result of capacity problems caused by there being only two chipping facilities in operation. The problem is that drivers have had to wait in line because they cannot effectively determine which line they should pull their trucks into. When drivers look down the roads to the two chipping facilities, they can estimate which facility has the smaller volume of pulpwood that remains to be processed, and they go to that facility.

Unfortunately, the pulpwood that remains to be processed at the selected facility could be of a species of trees that will require a longer time for processing than the larger volume pulpwood at the other facility. There is no way for a driver to estimate the mix of tree species that are waiting for processing at a chipping facility and estimate the amount of remaining time for processing. Given the required distance between the placement of the individual chipping facilities and the protective safety barriers that are in place, the driver cannot move to the other chipping facility if it becomes idle while they are still waiting in line at the facility that they originally selected.

Under Option 2, the current delivery process would be modified. The same trucks routinely make deliveries to the chipping operation, and previously recorded unloaded weights are known for each truck. The unloaded weight of any truck will vary during different deliveries, depending on a number of factors, such as the weight of different drivers who might be driving a given truck and the amount of fuel that is in the gas tanks at any time. However, the unloaded weight of any delivery truck can easily be estimated to within several hundred pounds from previous records. Any difference between the estimated unloaded weight and the actual unloaded weight of a given truck for a given delivery is almost inconsequential when compared to the weight of the pulpwood that is being carried. Once a truck has been weighed upon arrival at the yard office, a good estimate of the net weight of pulpwood on the load can therefore be obtained.

The members of the FPA cooperative will still require precise estimates of the weight of pulpwood that is being delivered by each truck, so the trucks will still be weighed both when they arrive and when they leave. The difference under this option is that the yard office will direct the driver to the specific chipping facility that has the least remaining processing time for pulpwood that must still be processed. This can be accomplished quite easily since it is known that the chippers can process about the same number of tons of pulpwood per hour, regardless of the species of wood that is being processed. They can process much larger volumes of fir trees than spruce trees per hour, but they will process about the same amount of weight of each type of tree per hour. As a result, the estimated weight of pulpwood on each load can be used to obtain a good estimate of the processing time at the chipping facility for the load.

The yard office will have a system to track the arrival times for each truck, the estimated processing time for each truck, and the specific chipping facility that each truck has been sent to. At any given time, this system will be able to indicate the remaining processing time at each chipping facility. When a delivery truck arrives, it will be weighed, have the load weight estimated, and be directed to the chipping facility with the least remaining processing time. If more than one facility is idle, the truck will be directed to the facility that has been idle the longest. Occasional idle times are not a problem for the chipping facilities since this permits routine periodic maintenance and cleanup to be performed.

It is not feasible to have trucks remain at the yard office to wait for directions as to which chipping facility they should go to when one of the facilities becomes open. This would cause some downtime at the chipping facilities while waiting for trucks to arrive from the yard office, and it could cause congestion near the scale when trucks are trying to be weighed at departure.

Option 3

All of the FPA members like the ideas from Option 2 and want to adopt them since they would be accomplished at a low cost and it seems that they would be very effective. However, some members think that there has also been a capacity issue at the chipper operation at the mill. They believe that the problem of having excess waiting time for drivers can only be resolved if a third chipping facility is added to the proposed chipping operation.

WAITING LINE QUESTIONS

The FPA members are still in the planning stages in trying to determine the wisdom of establishing their own cooperative chipping operation. If the proposed chipping operation is established, it will be run in effectively the same manner as the existing operation at the mill except for the modifications that are described in Option 2 and Option 3. They have found a good location to place such a facility near Fargo, New Hampshire. They are actively pursuing cost estimates to establish and operate such a facility, they are considering the best way to distribute all costs across cooperative members, and they are pursuing the possibilities for securing loans to establish the facility. The remaining question is the decision as to whether to go with Option 2 or with Option 3. The cost of adding and operating a third chipper facility to the proposed operation will be forthcoming, but a cost-benefit analysis can not be performed without some input on the impact that adding a third facility will have on waiting time for drivers.

The yard office at the mill was asked to provide FPA with information on recent days during which only timber companies that are associated with FPA made deliveries to the chipping operation. Other individual timber cutters, who are not FPA members, have periodically taken loads of pulpwood to the mill. The managers at the mill have been very cooperative with FPA during their transition out of the chipping operation, and such a day was identified. This was a typical operating day for both the timber companies and the chipping operation at the mill. FPA members delivered 35 loads of pulpwood to the chipping operation on that day. The FPA members gathered their copies of the billing tickets from the yard office for that day, and the results of interest are shown in Exhibit 9.1. Exhibit 9.1 gives the arrival time for each truck and its processing time after it pulled up to the chipping facility that serviced it. Service times are shown in minutes, and arrival times are shown in terms of the number of minutes that the particular truck arrived after the start of the 12-hour work shift at the chipping operation.

The arrival patterns in Exhibit 9.1 make sense to FPA membership. Drivers are typically unwilling to take fully loaded trucks long distances over mountain roads near the end of the workday at the chipping operation, risking the possibility of arriving with a

EXHIBIT 9.1
Arrival Times and Service Times (Minutes) for Deliveries at the Yard Office

Arrival Number	Arrival Time	Service Time	Arrival Number	Arrival Time	Service Time
0	0	0	18	297	23
1	2	42	19	343	25
2	5	30	20	387	56
3	7	48	21	398	54
4	21	46	22	400	35
5	43	43	23	419	59
6	45	22	24	441	57
7	58	24	25	472	50
8	102	25	26	473	43
9	127	37	27	493	59
10	154	39	28	512	52
11	156	48	29	565	61
12	171	21	30	586	52
13	179	52	31	608	57
14	216	48	32	613	19
15	232	31	33	645	31
16	246	35	34	654	29
17	248	22	35	682	25

fully loaded truck to find that the chipping operation is closed. In addition, the chipping operation stops accepting deliveries 30 minutes before the end of its 12-hour shift. If there is any perceived risk of arriving at the chipping operation after it stops accepting deliveries, fully loaded trucks are left at the landing where cutting is being done. The drivers then arrive early to get the loaded truck to the chipping operation when it opens the next day. This explains the larger than average number of arrivals at the opening of the chipping operation shift. There is no reason to assume that this behavior would change with the proposed FPA cooperative chipping operation.

We are interested in estimating the expected time that trucks would wait in line for service with Option 2 and Option 3, based on the results from Exhibit 9.1. Waiting line models can be used to determine the expected values of many different service characteristics in situations like the one being considered. However, it is necessary to determine the validity of any assumptions that are made with such models before they are used. The primary assumptions in waiting line models are concerned with the specific probability distributions that are used to describe both arrival patterns (Poisson distribution) and service time patterns (negative exponential distribution).

This type of analysis is quite removed from the background training of the FPA membership. They want to know if the standard assumptions behind typical waiting line models are valid for their situation. Given the results of that finding, they want estimates of the expected time that drivers would wait in line with Option 2 and Option 3. They are also interested in hearing any other suggestions that they might not be considering.*

---

*Technical note:** When verifying the validity of the waiting line assumptions, use expected arrival rates and service rates that are based on 30-minute time intervals.

AAA Products

AAA Products is a large industrial firm with many different facilities that specialize in the production of a number of end products, each of which has a high sales volume. The AAA facility that is currently being examined is primarily involved in the final assembly operation for one of these end products. Most of the components for this assembly operation come from outside sources. Some of the components are produced at other AAA facilities, and some are purchased from subcontractors. This assembly facility operates by processing the final end product in stages, as it passes sequentially through a large number of different workstations within the facility.

Each of the individual workstations contains some specialized equipment that is operated by a worker who is assigned to that specific workstation. Different sets of production and assembly steps are performed at each individual workstation in the sequence. The finished product is always processed in exactly the same sequence through the workstations. Batches of material are transferred from one workstation to the next workstation in the sequence on an as-needed basis. There is no concern about the order in which the individual items in an incoming batch are processed after they arrive at any given workstation. Material is shuttled between workstations for processing with a relatively labor-intense procedure, which costs AAA about $800/hr. during every operating hour. While this shuttling procedure is expensive, we shall see later that there are also some benefits that are associated with using it.

The amount of time it takes to complete the work performed at each of the workstations in the sequence of operations has been balanced in order to maintain a smooth workflow through the facility. There are, of course, periodic breakdowns at each of the workstations, which always create serious problems when they happen. The pattern of breakdowns is generally consistent over all of the different workstations, and Exhibit 10.1 summarizes historical evidence to describe this pattern of breakdowns. Maintenance records were checked for the last 1,000 hours of operation at the facility to determine the distribution of the reported number of workstation breakdowns per hour. These observations were all taken during normal operating conditions, and they can be assumed to represent typical breakdown behavior at

EXHIBIT 10.1 Observed Breakdowns per Hour for the Last 1,000 Hours of Operation

Number of Breakdowns	Observed Frequency
0	361
1	381
2	184
3	61
4	7
5	2
6	1
7	1
8	1
9	1

the facility. This particular AAA facility operates for a total of 50 weeks per year, with a standard 40-hour workweek, resulting in a total of 2,000 hours per year of operation.

Under the existing operating conditions at this facility, work continues at all of the remaining functioning workstations whenever a breakdown occurs. This situation causes interstage inventory to build up at workstations that are upstream from the breakdown location. It also allows for operations to continue at workstations that are downstream from the breakdown location. The downstream locations continue to function by using up the existing interstage inventory that built up at each respective location during previous breakdowns at other workstations. As a result, the workstations in this facility operate in such a manner that they can be considered to be working independently of all other workstations. This situation is also facilitated by the flexibility to maneuver components around as a result of the existing shuttling system for components.

The principle of having this independence between workstations has been considered to be quite worthwhile to AAA management since downtime costs are estimated to be $5,000/hr. for each workstation that is not operating. This cost is incurred both during the time in which repairs are being performed and during the time in which the workstation is awaiting service. There is also a significant cost that is associated with starting up any workstation once it has been shut down for any reason. This start-up cost is avoided when workstations continue to operate independently during breakdowns at other workstations, as described.

A maintenance crew at AAA performs equipment repairs when there are breakdowns at the workstations. The maintenance crew consists of two workers, a mechanic and an assistant, who go to workstations in a motorized cart to perform repairs as a team, as needed. That is, the two workers work together to repair one machine at a time. There is a large amount of testing and repair equipment in this motorized cart that this maintenance team must carry along with them at all times, since they never know which workstation they might be summoned to at any given time. The equipment that the current maintenance crew is using is due for replacement. The state of the equipment has not interfered with the operation of the maintenance crew to this point, but that problem would be expected to develop if the maintenance crew is not reequipped soon.

There is a one-time cost of $100,000 to initially equip a maintenance crew, and there is an additional cost of $200/hr. during each hour of operation to keep the maintenance crew operating. This additional cost covers all compensation for the two workers and all extra maintenance costs related to keeping the testing and repair equipment in good operating order. Both of these costs will be incurred to reequip the existing maintenance crew under any circumstances, and both of these costs would be incurred for each additional maintenance crew that AAA might set up for operation. There would be no incremental benefit from having any more than one maintenance crew working at the same workstation when a repair is required. The maintenance crew cannot perform any other useful function at times when they are not performing repairs, despite the fact that they will be paid, regardless of whether or not they are actually performing repairs at workstations. However, the high cost of downtime at a workstation makes the manager wonder if it is worthwhile to add an additional maintenance crew to the operating system.

Exhibit 10.2 gives some information about the distribution of repair times that it took for the existing maintenance crew to perform all repairs during the last 1,000 hours of operation at the AAA facility in question. Crew times at AAA have been reported in such a way that the repair times can only be reported in terms of one-tenth-hour intervals. For

EXHIBIT 10.2
Maintenance Crew Repair Times (in Hours) at AAA Workstations

Interval Start	Interval Finish	Observed Frequency
0.0	0.099	517
0.1	0.199	275
0.2	0.299	127
0.3	0.399	53
0.4	0.499	14
0.5	0.599	5
0.6	0.699	3
0.7	0.799	3
0.8	0.899	2
0.9	0.999	1

example, there were 275 repair calls from workstations that took between .1 and .199 hours for completion. The reported repair times in Exhibit 10.2 include the small amount of travel time that it took for the maintenance crew to get to the workstations for each of the reported breakdowns. Any additional maintenance crews that might be added to the system can be expected to perform service at about the same rate as the existing maintenance crew.

The manager of AAA wants some information regarding the financial impact of adding maintenance crews to the system, and knows that the analysis of this problem is reliant upon queuing theory. The manager is very comfortable with routine financial analysis, but has less than complete confidence in the application of quantitative models. As a result, we need to show some simple support for any assumptions that are being made about probability distributions. We can do this for arrivals by simultaneously plotting the observed distribution of the probability for the number of arrivals per hour along with the associated theoretical probability values that would have been observed with any assumed distribution for arrivals per hour. The same type of simultaneous plots can be performed for distributions of service times. However, there are some difficulties with this because of the way in which service times are reported in Exhibit 10.2.

It is reasonable to assume, for the purposes of arithmetic computation, that all service times within any interval have the midpoint service time for the interval while determining the overall expected time for service. However, when we develop any plots that are related to the distribution of actual observed probabilities for completion times, it is not reasonable to make the same assumption. We know only that all observations that are reported in any interval each have completion times that are above the starting point for the interval and below the ending point for the interval. All of the observations in any interval did not really take the interval average time for completion, and their times are actually spread out over the entire interval.

The $100,000 initial investment for the setup of each maintenance crew must be depreciated over an eight-year horizon for the project (14%, 25%, 17%, 13%, 9%, 9%, 9%, 4%). We want to know the total expected cost for this system, when the options of both one and two maintenance crews are considered. These expected costs should include all of the associated costs that have been mentioned above. In particular, the manager wants to know the net present value of all costs, accounting for taxes and depreciation, over the eight-year horizon for the project, using a 12% discount rate and a 35% tax rate. The initial expense will be made immediately, with all other after-tax costs and tax savings from depreciation being discounted at the end of their associated year. This analysis should lead to a conclusion regarding the advisability of adding a second maintenance crew to the system. This analysis ignores a number of real costs in the system, such as staffing costs for the workers at the workstations, supervisory costs, and the cost for materials. However, all of these costs are the same for any of the options that are being considered, and they will therefore have no impact on the relative comparisons of the options under consideration.

AUTOMATED MATERIAL HANDLING AT AAA?

The manager of AAA has started to think about the option of further modifying the operating system in this facility by changing the process for shuttling material between workstations. The obvious payoff for installing an automated material handling system to implement this process is substantial since the $800/hr. cost that is currently incurred for shuttling material between workstations would be completely eliminated. However, the costs for the implementation of such a system are also substantial since the initial expense for installation is estimated to be about $2,000,000, which would be depreciated over the eight-year horizon. Moreover, by linking all of the workstations in the sequence together with this automated handling process, the flexibility of maintaining independence in the system would be lost to a great degree. When such a system is implemented, it would cause all workstations in the system to be down whenever any workstation was not operating. Because of the high cost for starting up workstations that have been shut down for any reason, all functioning workstations would continue to run on an idle basis whenever any other workstation is shut down for repair. As a result, we can expect that the breakdown patterns for workstations with automated material handling would remain the same as in Exhibit 10.1. The addition of an automated handling system would also have no anticipated impact on the distribution of repair times that is given in Exhibit 10.2.

The addition of an automated handling system would result in substantial savings from not holding large amounts of interstage inventory between the workstations. However, the overall downtime cost will be substantially increased since the entire system is down if any workstation is not operating. It is estimated that downtime cost would be $9,000/hr. for all of the time that the entire system is not operating because any number of workstations are not operating. The manager of AAA wants to know the net present value of total cost, after accounting for taxes and depreciation, with the automated handling system in place, with the option of using one or two maintenance crews. The factors in the financial analysis of these options should remain the same as in the previous analysis. The earlier estimated costs that result from establishing maintenance crews will not change with the option of using an automated material handling system.*

---

*Technical note: When using multiple channel models for waiting lines with large source populations, Poisson arrival rates, and negative exponential service time, the following relationships can be used for precise calculations for the probability that there are no units in the system (P_0), the average number of units in the system ($\bar{n}_s$), and the average time spent in the system ($\bar{t}_s$) for M channels.

$$P_0 = \cfrac{1}{\displaystyle\sum_{i=0}^{M-1}\left[\frac{1}{i!}\left(\frac{\lambda}{\mu}\right)^i\right] + \frac{1}{M!}\left(\frac{\lambda}{\mu}\right)^M \frac{M\mu}{M\mu - \lambda}}$$

$$\bar{n}_s = \frac{\lambda\mu(\lambda/\mu)^M}{(M-1)!(M\mu - \lambda)^2}P_0 + \frac{\lambda}{\mu}$$

$$\bar{t}_s = \frac{\bar{n}_s}{\lambda}$$

If service times fit a negative exponential distribution, the cumulative probability that it will take time t, or longer, for completion is given by $e^{-\mu t}$, where μ is the expected service rate.

Supply Chain Management

McCloskey Office Supplies

McCloskey Office Supplies (MOS) is a firm that distributes a wide range of office supply products. The firm has approximately 20 retail outlets located in a large metropolitan area, along with a central storage facility. The firm operates by receiving all incoming products at the central storage facility, which then distributes items to the retail outlets. When delivery trucks make their frequent runs to take products from the central storage facilities to the outlets, they can also redistribute products between the retail outlets. That is, any retail outlet can inform the central storage facility at any time that they are running low on inventory of an item, and they are then resupplied from inventory at the central storage area. However, they might also be resupplied during a delivery run by switching some inventory from another retail outlet, which does have the product on hand, if the central storage facility is out of stock for the item. As a result, the entire inventory of all retail outlets and the central storage facility can be thought of as a single pool of inventory.

MOS management likes this process of moving products between stores since it tends to minimize the risk of stockouts at any location, except when demand for a product is high at all locations during an ordering cycle. Given the retail nature of the outlets, there are no "big buyers" of any of the products. MOS has many customers during a typical day, and almost all of these customers purchase things in small quantities.

MOS carries a wide variety of products and brands for items that it keeps in stock. Few of their customers have any strong brand loyalty, and it is quite common that customers will buy substitutes if there is a stockout of a specific brand of some product type. However, customer dissatisfaction might develop if some more popular brands of products are stocked out too frequently. The nature of the business gives a benchmark such that MOS should hold safety stock for each item that it carries to be 97.5% certain of getting through an order cycle without having a stockout of the item. Because of the substitution effect in purchasing, there will not be any significant number of "lost sales" as long as MOS maintains the benchmark standard of holding inventory to meet the 97.5% service level.

The MOS management group at the central storage facility does all of the ordering of products from outside suppliers. Under current policy, all products are ordered by using a fixed order period procedure, on a six-week order cycle. It is expensive to order in this situation since a count of products must be made at all of the retail outlets and at the central storage facility to get an accurate count of existing inventory before placing an order. MOS does maintain an ongoing inventory control count from sales records. However, a physical count must be made before placing an order to adjust the ongoing inventory counts for such things as theft, having items sold with the wrong UPC Code, and items that become damaged at the outlets and have to be discarded. All orders from suppliers arrive back at MOS in a single shipment, with no incremental deliveries.

Exhibit 11.1 shows the weekly demand over one year for a typical high-volume product that MOS sells. Due to the large volume of this product and the associated large inventory, it is expensive to go through a complete count for this product. MOS management estimates that it costs $525 every time an order is placed for this product and the resulting shipment is received, regardless of the size of the order. This cost includes charges for shipping. The unit cost to MOS for this particular item is $1, for any order quantity. That is, no price breaks are offered for ordering the product in large quantities.

MOS management wants to reevaluate their policy of six-week order cycles because of the high cost of placing orders. They realize that there is a trade-off in costs between ordering costs and holding costs. By extending the length of the order cycles, they will place fewer orders each year and thereby reduce annual ordering costs. However, there will be an increased cost for holding inventory. As order cycles get longer with fixed order period models, order quantities to cover expected usage during the order cycle also get larger, leading to higher inventory costs to cover the basic expected usage. In addition, longer order cycles will require increased levels of safety stock to maintain the 97.5% service level policy.

There is no precise value that MOS attaches to annual holding costs for inventory. However, their accounting office has gone through records for the last two years, and it has obtained some information that is related to obtaining the variable holding cost, as a percentage of the value of the item being held. The costs represent an accumulation over all products that MOS keeps in inventory, not just the product from Exhibit 11.1.

Last year, the average value of total inventory on hand, based on the cost of product to MOS, is estimated at $9,482,000. The total of all costs for holding inventory is estimated to

EXHIBIT 11.1
Weekly Demand for a Typical High-Volume MOS Product

Week	Demand	Week	Demand
1	14,319	27	28,807
2	14,004	28	14,151
3	14,957	29	13,875
4	15,392	30	31,217
5	14,044	31	11,636
6	29,058	32	19,810
7	15,287	33	19,556
8	15,808	34	20,995
9	29,072	35	29,990
10	15,964	36	25,938
11	12,951	37	29,209
12	24,600	38	24,507
13	37,786	39	7,651
14	19,996	40	13,485
15	5,490	41	33,889
16	16,187	42	26,165
17	21,858	43	30,313
18	19,194	44	16,344
19	18,615	45	11,443
20	20,342	46	20,095
21	20,976	47	17,376
22	14,710	48	15,127
23	21,540	49	19,492
24	23,141	50	16,769
25	29,493	51	25,641
26	10,126	52	21,609

have been $1,895,000 for that year. Some of these holding costs are fixed costs for such things as payments for funds that were borrowed a number of years ago to construct the central storage facility. Two years ago, the average value of total inventory was less, at an estimated value of $9,234,000. The total of all costs associated with holding inventory for that year was $1,865,000, which includes the same fixed costs as the other year mentioned above. None of the differences in these estimated annual costs is attributed to inflationary effects or to differences in interest that was incurred for funds that were used to pay for stock that was held in inventory,

The management of MOS wants estimates of the total expected annual costs for using various lengths of order cycles. The lead time for orders is two weeks for any order cycle length, and we wish to consider total expected costs for order cycles of 2, 3, 4, 5, 6, 7, and 8 weeks' duration for comparison purposes, given the information that has been provided about the existing situation. There are three components to total expected annual cost for these different ordering options. The first component is the expected annual cost for placing orders. The second component is the annual cost for carrying the basic inventory to meet expected demand during the order cycle. The third component is the expected annual cost for carrying additional safety stock.

It will be reasonable to assume that weekly demand is constant for the purposes of computing expected costs, with this relatively high service level. The expected order quantity for each cycle will then be equal to the expected usage during an order cycle. If demand were constant every week, then any safety stock would be carried as excess throughout the year with a fixed-order-period procedure. The amount of surplus safety stock that is remaining in inventory at the very end of order cycles will certainly vary. However, we will approximate the annual incremental holding cost for safety stock with the assumption that we will, on average, be carrying the safety stock quantity as excess inventory throughout the year in order to maintain the required target service level. MOS is in operation 52 weeks per year.

Given all of this information, the MOS manager wants to see a summary that presents the expected total annual cost for using order cycles of 2, 3, 4, 5, 6, 7, and 8 weeks' duration. This total cost should include ordering costs, holding cost for basic inventory, and the incremental cost for carrying safety stock to meet a 97.5% service level.

Burton's Wine Cellar

Burton's Wine Cellar (BWC) is a very large retail outlet that caters to wine enthusiasts. The store carries an extensive variety of different types and brands of wine. The bulk of the volume of the store is based on the sale of "value wine," which satisfies the quality standards of most wine drinkers, while being sold at a moderate price level. The store also carries many different types and brands of relatively exclusive wines to accommodate the tastes of their more discerning consumers. BWC prides itself on the breadth of its extensive inventory. Many customers arrive at the store to browse through the selection that is available and then select a brand that appeals to them while they are shopping in the store. Some brands are occasionally stocked out. However, the very knowledgeable sales staff on the floor can almost always direct customers who might be specifically seeking a particular brand that is stocked out to some other brand that is similar to what they were originally seeking. Because of this brand substitution effect, there is hardly ever an instance of a totally lost sale that results from occasional stockouts of brands of wine. Customers typically do not buy any one brand in large quantities when making a purchase at the store.

The management of BWC is well aware of the fact that routine stockouts of some of the more popular brands could ultimately lead to customer dissatisfaction and to some lost sales. The general nature of the business is such that BWC management has an established benchmark policy, such that they wish to maintain inventory at a level to be 95% confident that they will get through the order cycle for any given brand without having any stockouts for that particular brand. BWC should not expect to incur any significant levels of lost sales, as long as the 95% service level policy is maintained, given the general standards of this business.

The very large number of different brands carried by BWC has led management to use a fixed-order-period model for replenishment of inventory, rather than to be involved with perpetual ordering systems. BWC maintains a running inventory count from sales records, but periodic physical inventory counts are required to adjust and to update these records. Differences between this running count and actual inventory levels result primarily from breakage of bottles, since theft is minimized by a very strict security system that is reinforced by the presence of sales staff on the floor. Tight control of inventory is critical for BWC, due to all of the many legal issues that are involved with the sale of alcoholic beverages. Because of this, it is not feasible to consider any reordering option that would allow for more than eight weeks between physical inventory counts. The physical counts must be very accurate.

Shelves in the store are kept fully stocked, whenever possible, so customers will not erroneously conclude that the store is running out of different brands. The bottles for this routine restocking of shelves come from a large storage room in the back of the building that is used to hold much of the total inventory that is maintained. This situation makes precise inventory counting quite difficult. The specific problem is that the wide variety of brands that are sold leads to many small quantities of some lower-volume brands being stored together in cardboard boxes, to minimize the total requirement for storage space. All of these boxes must therefore be opened, and each bottle checked, to be assured that the correct brand is being accounted for during these physical counts. This physical counting of inventory is a very time-consuming process. In addition, the follow-up ordering procedure is also quite complicated, and finding adequate shipping that is secure for bottled alcoholic beverages is expensive. BWC management estimates that it costs an average of $125 for each individual order for a given brand of wine to be placed, to be shipped, and to be received back at BWC. Each individual order arrives back at BWC in single-lot shipments, not in incremental deliveries.

BWC will definitely place orders whenever inventory records are updated after a physical count of inventory has been performed. There are serious concerns about the frequency with which these physical counts should be done. If longer order cycles are used, then larger orders must be placed each time to cover the basic expected usage during the cycle, which will increase the average value of inventory that is being held during the year. If longer order cycles are used, then larger amounts of safety stock will also be required to meet the established benchmark service level. However, longer order cycles will reduce the number of orders that are placed, and the ordering costs are quite expensive. Management wants some input on the total expected annual cost for holding inventory for various feasible order cycle lengths.

The manager of BWC specifically wants estimates of the total expected annual combined cost for carrying basic inventory to meet expected demand, for the expected cost of carrying additional safety stock to meet the benchmark service level, and for the total cost for placing orders. Any fixed-annual-cost components of inventory holding cost can be ignored since they will have no impact on the relative comparison of total expected annual cost for various lengths of order cycles. It is feasible to consider using order cycles of 4, 5, 6, 7 or 8 weeks. The lead time for order will be two weeks for any order cycle.

Estimates of holding costs are more difficult to obtain than the stated ordering cost given above. In order to be able to perform analyses for all of the different brands that are carried, we need some measure of the annual unit variable holding cost as a percentage of the value of the item that is being held in inventory. That is, a percentage that is based on the cost of product to BWC. The accountant for BWC was contacted for input regarding inventory holding costs, and some old sales and tax records have been examined. It was found that the average value of total inventory for all products that were held last year, not just the particular product that will be under consideration later, was approximately $2,327,000, and the total of all inventory-related expenses for all products was $1,886,000. Some of the inventory-related expenses include substantial fixed-cost outlays, including things like the repayment of loans for the original construction of the store. The overall value of total inventory was lower during the previous year, with a total average value of $2,119,00 with an associated total inventory related cost value of $1,861,000. The fixed-cost components of inventory-related costs were approximately equal over both years, and economic conditions and interest rates have been very stable over the associated two-year period.

The weekly demand for bottles of a typical product, of the hundreds of products held by BWC, is given in Exhibit 12.1 for the past year. There are no obvious trends in weekly usage. The BWC cost for acquiring this particular product is $6 per unit for any order quantity, and we wish to know the order cycle length that should be used to minimize total combined expected annual inventory cost for this product under existing circumstances. BWC operates 52 weeks per year.

With the reasonably high service level that is being considered, it will be acceptable to assume that weekly demand is constant for the purposes of computing expected costs. The expected order quantity for each cycle will then be equal to the expected usage during an order cycle. The impact of carrying safety stock can be more difficult to precisely determine on a cost basis. The amount of safety stock that is remaining in inventory at the very end of any particular order cycle will certainly vary, and that amount would have been carried in excess throughout that order cycle. We will approximate the annual incremental holding cost for safety stock with the assumption that we will, on average, be carrying the safety stock quantity as excess inventory throughout the year in order to maintain the required target service level.

The manager of BWC specifically wants a summary of estimates of the total expected annual combined cost for various order cycle lengths. This total cost includes the cost for carrying the basic inventory required to meet expected demand, the expected cost of carrying additional safety stock to meet the benchmark service level, and the total cost for placing orders. These costs should be obtained for the options of using order cycles of each of 4, 5, 6, 7, and 8 weeks. Of primary interest are the determination of the least cost order cycle length and some input on the sensitivity of this total cost to changes in order cycle length.

BWC management is also very aware of the fact that the determination of the optimal length for order

EXHIBIT 12.1
Weekly
Demand for
a Typical
BWC Product

Week	Demand	Week	Demand
1	519	27	519
2	614	28	461
3	469	29	458
4	473	30	632
5	460	31	436
6	610	32	516
7	472	33	608
8	478	34	525
9	610	35	619
10	479	36	580
11	421	37	623
12	566	38	376
13	697	39	394
14	463	40	454
15	565	41	659
16	481	42	581
17	538	43	623
18	511	44	483
19	506	45	434
20	523	46	534
21	529	47	493
22	467	48	471
23	535	49	514
24	551	50	507
25	460	51	558
26	449	52	536

cycles could change over time. This would result if the variable component of annual unit holding cost changes with such factors as the interest rate that is charged for money that is borrowed to hold inventory. If variable holding costs decline, the option of using longer order cycles, with their associated larger inventory levels, becomes more feasible. BWC management wants to know the ranges of annual variable holding cost values for which each of the 4-, 5-, 6-, 7-, and 8-week order cycles would be the least total expected annual cost option for the particular product described above. These variable holding cost values should be stated in terms of a percent of value of the item being stored.

Guzzo Pharmacies, Inc.

Guzzo Pharmacies, Inc. (GPI), is located in a large city, and it consists of a number of retail drugstores that are supplied by the firm's central distribution center that does all ordering from outside suppliers. Inventory is maintained at the central distribution center for most items that the retail stores carry, but the primary focus of concern at the moment is the management of the inventory of prescription drugs for the pharmacies that are located inside each of the GPI retail outlets. The inventory of this particular line of products is obviously maintained under extremely tight control at both the central distribution center and at the pharmacies. The pharmacies are regularly resupplied by a company shuttle van in order to ensure that they are fully stocked. It is considered completely unacceptable for a pharmacy to be stocked out of any prescription drug for any significant period of time.

If a given pharmacy location does ever stock out of a particular prescription drug, it can be resupplied from the central distribution center during a regularly scheduled run by the shuttle van in a relatively short period of time. GPI considers it barely acceptable to occasionally have to tell customers that there will be a delay of a few hours in filling a prescription due to a stockout, that they can accept partially filled prescriptions with the remainder being available the next day, or that they can alternatively obtain the prescription at another nearby GPI branch. But prolonged delays of more than a few hours are considered totally unacceptable both to GPI management and to GPI customers. If the central distribution center is also stocked out of a particular item, then some inventory from another GPI pharmacy can be transferred by the shuttle van to the given pharmacy that has stocked out.

A running count of the inventory of all prescription drugs is immediately updated from any GPI sales transaction that involves a prescription drug. These running counts are quite accurate, since the tight security that surrounds the sale of prescription drugs largely eliminates the possibility of theft by customers. Pharmacists are also rotated around to different GPI locations on a regular basis to avoid any conceivable possibility that they might be colluding in the theft of these drugs from the inventory at any pharmacy. Physical counts of inventory are conducted frequently at every pharmacy to ensure that the running counts are accurate.

Since GPI maintains very accurate records of its prescription drug inventory at all times, it is a natural situation for them to use a fixed-order-quantity ordering system. Exhibit 13.1 shows weekly sales records from the past year for prescriptions of a typical product that GPI carries in its inventory. This product is a commonly prescribed

EXHIBIT 13.1
Weekly Sales
for a Typical
GPI Product

Week	Demand	Week	Demand
1	234	27	381
2	316	28	225
3	243	29	171
4	415	30	377
5	225	31	188
6	441	32	306
7	243	33	398
8	252	34	324
9	419	35	459
10	252	36	396
11	207	37	141
12	378	38	378
13	567	39	135
14	243	40	216
15	99	41	425
16	261	42	385
17	342	43	399
18	297	44	261
19	288	45	189
20	225	46	400
21	323	47	279
22	234	48	143
23	333	49	399
24	360	50	177
25	450	51	302
26	224	52	275

steroid-based drug that is sold in most pharmacies. Each individual prescription of this particular drug is sold as a self-contained packet, and each packet contains the same number of tablets. Only one of these packets is ever sold at one time to any customer. The data in Exhibit 13.1 shows no observable patterns from seasonality or trend in the demand for this drug.

GPI management wants the central distribution center to continue using a fixed-order-quantity policy for ordering prescription drug inventory from its sources. This policy should be helpful in minimizing the combined expected cost of ordering and holding inventory to account for its normal expected usage. This policy makes sense since GPI has a good estimate of existing inventory on hand for prescription drugs at all times.

It is estimated that it costs about $165 to go through the process of placing and receiving an order every time an order is placed under normal circumstances, regardless of the size of the order. Since the physical volume of the product is small, shipping costs are quite small. When orders are placed under normal circumstances, the cost of the particular product in Exhibit 13.1 is $28.60/prescription to GPI, and there is a two-week lead time for all shipments to arrive. It is possible for GPI to place emergency orders to obtain small quantities of the product in an overnight delivery, but that becomes very expensive, as we shall see later.

Some accounting records have been searched to obtain information about the annual variable holding costs for prescription drugs as a percentage of the value of the item being held. This variable holding cost is primarily driven by interest GPI must pay on outstanding loans it holds to pay for buying the products it holds in inventory. The interest rate has been quite stable for the past few years, and there are other variable costs that GPI incurs from holding inventory of these prescription drugs.

Last year the company spent a total of $1,896,000 on inventory-related expenses for all of their prescription drugs, not just for the selected product in Exhibit 13.1, while the associated average value of inventory being held was $5,483,000, based on the cost of product to GPI. During the previous year, $1,866,000 was spent on inventory-related expenses to hold an average value of inventory of $5,243,000. These estimates of inventory-related expenses for prescription drugs include some fixed-cost components, for such things as additional security required at the central distribution center because of the large quantities of these inventoried prescription drugs. This cost is fixed since the same level of security is always required, regardless of the value of the prescription drugs being secured at any given time.

The precise accuracy of the ongoing count of remaining inventory will give GPI a clear advanced warning of the possibility that the entire GPI system might be on the verge of stocking out of any given prescription drug during the normal two-week lead time for an order. All orders arrive from suppliers in a single shipment, so there is no incremental delivery. GPI operates 52 weeks per year.

If GPI learns that a systemwide stockout is about to happen, they can place an emergency order from their supplier to receive a small quantity of the needed item with an overnight delivery. Large quantities of product cannot be delivered in this fashion, but GPI can get enough of the product through these means to get them through the remaining days of an order cycle. The cost of this service is expensive, with an associated penalty cost of $625 every time that it happens.

GPI management wants an analysis of the financial impact of using different inventory policies, with an emphasis on the effect of considering different service level policies. Service levels for a given product are defined in terms of the probability that GPI will get through a complete order cycle without stocking out of that product. Some annual cost is associated with holding inventory and placing orders to meet the expected demand during the year. This annual cost can be estimated as the cost that would be obtained with the assumption of constant usage, since only relatively high service levels will be considered. This cost will remain the same for any specified service level.

The issue of dealing with the expected cost for carrying additional safety stock can become quite complicated. However, any safety stock quantity will always be present in excess of expected usage at the reorder point in a fixed-order-quantity model. If we assume constant usage during the lead time, the safety stock quantity will still be there at the end of the lead time. With variable usage, sometimes there will be more, and sometimes less, left at the end of the two-week lead time. We make an approximation by assuming that the safety stock amount will be remaining in excess in inventory, on average, at the end of the lead time. This excess will then be present when the order quantity arrives, so that starting inventory for each cycle will, on average, have the safety stock amount in excess at the start of each order cycle. As a result, this safety stock will, on average, be carried in excess throughout each order cycle.

By carrying additional safety stock, additional holding costs will be incurred by GPI. Higher service levels will require carrying greater levels of safety stock, thereby incurring higher costs for holding that safety stock. However, the resulting probability that a systemwide stockout will occur during an order cycle will be reduced with higher service levels, which reduces the associated probability that the penalty cost of an emergency order will be incurred.

In order to investigate the financial impact of different safety stock policies, GPI management wants to consider policies of 90%, 91%, 92%, 93%, 94%, 95%, 96%, 97%, 98%, and 99% service levels. These policies should be evaluated on the basis of total expected annual cost, which includes: cost of holding basic inventory for expected usage, cost of placing orders for basic expected usage, cost of holding safety stock, and expected penalty costs for emergency orders. From this information, GPI management can determine the service level option with the least total annual cost. The associated cost sensitivity from shifting to other service levels can also be observed.

QUANTITY DISCOUNT OPTIONS

GPI management has long been aware of the possibility of obtaining price breaks for ordering in large standard-shipment quantities from their suppliers. However, the amount of these discounts has not seemed adequate to consider that option since the required order quantities are quite large. For the particular product that we have been considering, a 1.5% price reduction is offered for order quantities of 3,000 units. The lead time for placing such orders would remain the same, and the option would still be open to obtain emergency overnight deliveries. GPI has sufficient demand for the product so that buying in such quantities would never lead to having the labeled expiration date reached while the product is still in inventory.

There is the reduction in the unit cost for acquiring the product, and GPI does purchase the product in large amounts over the course of a year. There would also be an associated reduction in the unit holding cost. GPI management would like to see the same type of cost analysis that was performed above repeated for the situation in which the price break is offered. Policies of 90%, 91%, 92%, 93%, 94%, 95%, 96%, 97%, 98%, and 99% service levels should be considered for this option. The results should be compared to the costs from the earlier analysis. Obviously, the total expected annual cost for these policies would now have to include the price of acquiring the product.

Dumala Electronic Supply

Dumala Electronic Supply (DES) is a small firm that is in the business of supplying electronic components to a number of different producers of end products. They are purely in the business of supplying other customers and do not produce anything themselves. DES has a number of major customers as the source of their business, and they are on very good terms with all of them, based on their reputation of many years of loyal customer service and a very competitive pricing strategy. Their customers typically make frequent purchases of products with small quantities being involved in each particular purchase.

For a firm that is driven by supplying components for very technologically advanced businesses, DES itself is seriously in need of some help in the way that it analyzes its own business practices. Existing practices at DES could be described as being a bit dated. This realization has led DES management to have some concerns that are centered on minimizing their own operating costs in order to facilitate the continuation of their strategy of maintaining a very competitive pricing posture while increasing profit margins to more acceptable levels. Of particular interest at this point is a cost-based analysis of their existing practices for holding inventory.

A great deal of information has been gathered by DES management in order to perform this cost-based analysis. As a first step, a typical product was selected to serve as the basis for the analysis. There are neither seasonal effects nor significant trend components in any of the items that DES keeps in inventory, as with the selected product. Sales records were searched to determine the weekly demand for this particular product for the past year. The results of this search are summarized in Exhibit 14.1.

The product in Exhibit 14.1 shows some variation in weekly demand, without having particularly wild variation. Again, this particular product exhibits typical behavior for the demand of all DES components held in inventory. Also, a number of inventory-related cost factors have been obtained from accounting and financial records.

Every time an order request is processed for the sample item, an inventory check is made to be sure that an order really is needed. Then the supplier is contacted and the order is placed. There is a three-week lead time between placing the order and receiving it. Shipments arrive in a single-lot delivery, with no incremental delivery. Once the shipment arrives, it is inspected and put away if it meets conformance quality standards.

EXHIBIT 14.1
Weekly Demand for a Typical DES Product

Week	Demand	Week	Demand
1	2,824	27	2,855
2	2,687	28	2,840
3	3,054	29	3,398
4	2,195	30	1,937
5	2,877	31	3,152
6	2,850	32	2,655
7	2,662	33	2,796
8	2,996	34	2,687
9	3,067	35	3,054
10	3,652	36	2,467
11	2,790	37	2,867
12	2,529	38	2,860
13	2,912	39	2,662
14	2,905	40	2,896
15	2,890	41	3,301
16	3,270	42	3,748
17	1,861	43	2,690
18	3,102	44	2,679
19	2,655	45	3,012
20	2,843	46	2,509
21	2,509	47	2,608
22	2,608	48	2,669
23	2,619	49	3,195
24	3,195	50	2,454
25	2,399	51	2,462
26	2,492	52	2,704

Otherwise, the shipment is returned, which creates all kinds of problems when it happens, but it happens very infrequently. The estimated cost of this procedure is $2,580 every time an order is placed when there are no returns. The product is quite compact and lightweight, so shipping costs account for only a small amount of this total. Most of this ordering cost results from an expensive process that is required to set things up for testing the components when the shipment arrives at DES. As a result, this cost for placing an order is effectively fixed for any order quantity.

The cost to DES for this item is $14.55 per unit, and no quantity discounts are available from the supplier. Many fixed costs are associated with holding inventory, but these have no effect on the relative evaluation of different inventory policies, so we will ignore them in our analysis. The primary component of variable holding cost is interest that DES pays on loans to cover the acquisition costs for products. The accountant for the firm has suggested that the annual variable holding cost for any component should be assessed as 12% of the acquisition cost for the component. DES operates 52 weeks every year.

EVALUATING FIXED-ORDER-PERIOD INVENTORY POLICIES

As mentioned before, DES management wants to see a cost-based analysis of its inventory policies. Records indicate that DES has maintained a 98.5% service level coverage for its customers. That is, orders have been met from inventory on hand throughout complete order cycles during 98.5% of the order cycles that have been observed. DES wants to be assured of maintaining this service level in any inventory policies that are being considered. Because this service level is so high, DES effectively never loses a sale. Customers will typically accept a substitute product in the rare event that a stockout occurs, or they will wait until a new shipment arrives, at which time DES staff will immediately deliver it. The policy of maintaining very competitive pricing, along with the high service level, keeps DES customers very loyal.

In keeping with the past practice with which they are very familiar, DES management wants to start out by evaluating the feasible fixed-order-period inventory models.

It is possible to consider order cycles in the range of three- through eight-weeks' duration. There are significant cost trade-offs as the length of order cycles increase. If DES uses longer order cycles, then more units must be purchased each time an order is placed to cover the basic expected usage during the cycle. This will increase the average value of inventory being held during the year. If DES uses longer order cycles, then larger amounts of safety stock will also be required to meet the established benchmark service level. However, longer order cycles will reduce the number of orders that are placed, and the ordering costs are quite expensive. Management wants some input on the total expected annual cost for holding inventory for the feasible order cycle lengths that have been specified. The manager of DES specifically wants estimates of the total expected annual combined cost for carrying basic inventory to meet expected demand, for the expected cost of carrying additional safety stock to meet the benchmark service level, and for the total cost for placing orders.

We can approximate the expected annual cost of ordering and holding inventory for basic expected usage by assuming that there is constant demand every week. However, the issue of dealing with the expected incremental cost for carrying safety stock can become very complicated, so we approximate this cost by making some assumptions. If weekly demand were constant, then any safety stock amount of inventory would be left in excess at the end of every order cycle. With variable weekly demand, sometimes there will be more and sometimes there will be less remaining in excess at the end of each order cycle. With the relatively high service level that DES is using, we will approximate the incremental cost of carrying additional safety stock by assuming that, on average, this safety stock amount is carried in excess throughout all order cycles.

DES management wants to receive a financial summary of the total expected annual cost values, as described above, for fixed-order-period inventory systems for each option of using three- through eight-week order cycles. It is of particular interest to determine the order cycle duration that minimizes this total expected annual cost. With this summary, it will also be possible to observe the financial sensitivity of this decision to changes over the range of feasible order cycle lengths.

OPTIONS FOR IMPROVEMENTS IN INVENTORY CONTROL

The use of fixed-order-period inventory models with long order cycles can lead to the requirement that large amounts of safety stock must be held to maintain high customer service levels. This naturally leads to a situation in which high incremental inventory holding costs are incurred for carrying that safety stock. Perpetual inventory systems keep much tighter records regarding the amount of inventory on hand, and safety stock must be carried to account only for variation during the lead time, not for variation during the entire order cycle. This results in the need to carry less safety stock to obtain the same customer service level.

DES management wants an estimate of the total expected annual cost for carrying the product from Exhibit 14.1, using a perpetual inventory system with the same 98.5% customer service level. Following the analysis from above, the expected cost for placing orders and for holding inventory to cover expected usage can be approximated with the assumption of constant usage.

As before, the issue of dealing with the expected incremental cost for carrying additional safety stock can become quite complicated. However, any safety stock quantity will always be present in excess of expected usage at the reorder point in a perpetual model. With the assumption of constant usage during the lead time, the safety stock quantity will still be there at the end of the lead time. When weekly demand is variable during the lead time, sometimes there will be more, and sometimes less, left at the end of the three-week lead time. We make an approximation by assuming that the safety stock amount will be remaining in excess in inventory, on average, when the order quantity arrives. The starting inventory for each cycle will then, on average, have the safety stock amount in excess at the start of each order cycle. As a result, this safety stock will, on average, be carried in excess throughout each order cycle.

Since less safety stock will have to be carried with the perpetual system, we should anticipate that it will have a lower expected total annual cost than was observed for the optimal fixed-order-period system. Unfortunately, perpetual systems require a fairly precise knowledge of the amount of inventory on hand at all times, and this knowledge must come at some cost.

The management of DES has done some investigation to determine what kind of a system they would need in order to maintain much tighter control over inventory, in the sense of having a much more accurate running count of inventory on hand. This would involve using a bar-coding system on all components that are stored, so as to track every component in the system. Scanners would have to be installed in strategic locations to monitor inventory flow, and a software system would have to be installed to update inventory records both as shipments arrive and as sales transactions take place.

This new inventory control system has an estimated expense of $235,000, which must ultimately be paid for from savings in operating costs that result from its use. Based on the analysis from above, the savings that result from using this system with the selected item in Exhibit 14.1 can be estimated. The DES accountant has done an analysis to estimate that the cost savings associated with this particular component represent about 3% of the total savings that DES would realize by extending this system over all of the components in its inventory. The system will be depreciated over the eight-year horizon for this project (14%, 25%, 17%, 13%, 9%, 9%, 9%, 4%). The initial expense would be incurred immediately.

The after-tax savings from having the system in operation would be equivalent to cash inflow, as would the tax benefits from depreciation. DES pays taxes at a rate of 35%. Except for the initial expense, all cash flows should be discounted to the end of their respective years for each year of the eight-year horizon. DES management wants to know the internal rate of return that would result from this $235,000 capital investment. This is considered to be a major investment by DES management, and they also want to know about any other additional factors related to acquiring this system that might be helpful to making a final decision.

Susmarski Smoke Detector Co.

Susmarski Smoke Detector Company (SSDC) produces two models of high-quality smoke detector units, among many other products, and it uses Material Requirements Planning (MRP) and Capacity Requirements Planning (CRP) in the process. Both of these units would more accurately be described as fire detectors, since they react to more than just smoke during a fire. In particular, both units will react to excessive heat. The basic unit reacts to both smoke and heat, so it is most effective at detecting smoldering fires, which produce significant levels of smoke. The deluxe unit will also react to the presence of excessive amounts of ionized material in the air, which makes it more capable of detecting burning fires, which do not produce as much smoke.

All smoke detector units are assembled at SSDC's assembly facility. Some components are purchased from outside vendors, and a department within SSDC manufactures some of the components. The basic model (denoted as part number A1) is assembled from two subassemblies: a base subassembly (A10) and a cover subassembly (A11). The A10 and A11 subassemblies are put together by a snap fit to produce an A1, and the process requires no additional parts. The A10 subassembly is produced in batches, and it is stored until it is needed for a production run of A1s. The A10 is assembled from an A100 subassembly and components A101 and A102. The A100 subassembly is produced in batches in an earlier step, and it is then stored until it is needed for a production run of one either one of SSDC's smoke detectors. The A100 is produced by taking an A1000 plastic frame unit and using a forced fit to attach an A1001 circuit board to it, so no additional parts are required for this step. The A1001 circuit board is purchased from an outside supplier with a very loud audio alarm already attached to it. The assembly of the A10 uses a previously assembled A100 and attaches both an A101 heat detector and an A102 smoke detector to the circuit board in the A100 unit. The A101 and A102 components are attached to the A100 subassembly by a soldering process that requires no additional parts when assembling an A10. The cover subassembly (A11) is produced from two components: a plastic cover unit (A103) and an identifying self-adhesive plate (A104) that is attached to the cover unit. The A1 unit is powered by batteries that, as might be guessed, are not supplied by SSDC. The material structure tree for an A1 is shown in Exhibit 15.1.

EXHIBIT 15.1
Material Structure Trees for A1 and A2

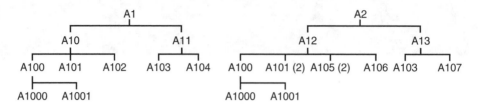

SSDC's deluxe model smoke detector (A2) is significantly more sophisticated than the basic A1 unit. The A2 includes backup components for added security, contains the more reliable ion detectors, and has a lighting unit that comes on when the alarm is activated. The A2 is assembled in a manner similar to that of the A1 unit, but it contains more components. The A2 unit is produced by using a snap fit to put together two subassemblies: an A12 base unit and an A13 cover unit. The A12 base unit is put together in the same fashion as the A10 base unit, by taking a previously assembled A100 subassembly and attaching two A101 heat detector components, two A105 ion detector components, and an A106 lighting unit to the circuit board in the A100 subassembly. The A13 cover assembly contains two components: an A103 plastic cover unit and an A107 self-adhesive identification plate. The A2 unit is directly hard-wired into the home by the consumer or the builder. A material structure tree for an A2 is shown in Exhibit 15.1.

Forecasted demand values for both A1 and A2 are shown in Exhibit 15.2 for each month of the next year.

Items that are assembled by SSDC (A1, A2, A10, A11, A12, A13, and A100) can be produced with a minimal setup cost and they can be produced in lots of any quantity. SSDC has many other uses for the assembly site, and there is a one-month lead time required for a run of any of these subassemblies. However, lot-for-lot shipment sizes can easily be provided. Multiple runs of different assembled items can be done in the facility during the same month.

Three components that are manufactured by a separate department at a different location within SSDC (A101, A102, and A105) are produced at a much slower rate than assembled units. A101, A102, and A105 components are manufactured at daily rates of 4,000 units/day, 3,000 units/day, and 2,000 units/day, respectively, when they are being produced, and they can not be produced concurrently. All three components are produced on the same assembly line at SSDC's manufacturing facility, and a changeover must be made to the line whenever a different component is to be run. The costs for changeovers at the manufacturing facility are significant, as shown in Exhibit 15.3. A two-month lead time is required for the manufactured components, which are produced during the first month of the lead time. Testing and shipping takes place during the second month of the lead time.

EXHIBIT 15.2
Forecasted Demand for A1 and A2 Smoke Detector Units

Month	A1	A2
Jan.	19,000	9,000
Feb.	17,000	7,000
Mar.	11,000	5,000
Apr.	9,000	3,500
May	6,000	3,000
June	6,000	2,000
July	5,000	1,500
Aug.	5,000	1,000
Sep.	5,000	3,000
Oct.	9,000	4,000
Nov.	9,000	4,500
Dec.	13,000	5,000

EXHIBIT 15.3 Acquisition and Inventory Information for SSDC Components

Item	Current Inventory	How Obtained	Lead Time	Setup Cost	Annual Holding Cost
A1	24,000	Assembly	1		
A2	14,000	Assembly	1		
A10	16,000	Assembly	1		
A11	19,000	Assembly	1		
A12	6,500	Assembly	1		
A13	9,000	Assembly	1		
A100	12,000	Assembly	1		
A101	27,000	Manufacture	2	$2,590	$3.50
A102	24,500	Manufacture	2	$2,820	$3.40
A103	29,000	Purchase	3	$455	$.07
A104	24,000	Purchase	2	$510	$.01
A105	10,500	Manufacture	2	$4,150	$10.10
A106	5,500	Purchase	2	$620	$.25
A107	8,000	Purchase	2	$178	$.01
A1000	21,000	Purchase	2	$520	$.10
A1001	20,000	Purchase	2	$840	$1.07

This testing phase is very important to SSDC since the firm is committed to producing a quality product that has the potential to save lives.

The manufacturing site operates five days per week, with an average of four weeks per month (SSDC operates 240 working days per year, and these are the only days during which components are required). The manufacturing site never operates on an overtime basis, and due to other commitments within SSDC, only 50% of its operating time within any given month can be used to meet the needs of producing components for smoke detectors. If two runs of A101, two runs of A102, or two runs of A105 are made within the same month, they can be run consecutively, and the initial setup cost will not be incurred for the second run.

If the 50% capacity limit of the manufacturing facility is exceeded in any month for the total requirements for A101, A102, and A105 components, a production run of one of them can be moved back to the previous month. Additional holding costs will be incurred for keeping the lot in inventory for an additional month, but a setup cost could be eliminated if the component that is shifted is already scheduled for production in the previous month. There are difficulties with producing components earlier than is required because the manufacturing facility has limited storage space. Shifting a production run back more than one month is not practical. The process of moving production runs back to the month before they are scheduled will only be considered for months when the 50% capacity restriction will be violated with desired scheduling from MRP.

All other components are purchased from outside vendors. Lot sizes for all manufactured and purchased items are obtained by appropriate Economic Order Quantity (EOQ) relationships to minimize the total relevant cost. All necessary information for obtaining EOQs for components is given in Exhibit 15.3. In obtaining EOQ order sizes, lot sizes should be rounded to the nearest multiple of 500 units (round up or down to the nearest multiple of 500 units). Exhibit 15.3 also gives lead times and initial inventories for all components and subassemblies.

Excess inventories of assembled items have accumulated because previous actual monthly demand was less than forecasted demand, from random effects. The existence of excess current inventories should not influence our estimates of annual demand for EOQ calculations, so annual-demand estimates for components should be based on the predicted annual demand for A1 and A2, and existing inventories should be ignored. Any excess accumulated inventory will be used up before any more orders are placed, and the business will then continue on an ongoing basis with the expected annual demand values.

The manager of SSDC wants to develop an MRP schedule for all of the components for a production schedule for A1 and A2 to meet forecasted demand for the next year. Due to variability in forecasts, the scheduled ending inventory for each of A1 and A2 in each month should be 25% of the forecasted demand for the following month. The resulting MRP must not be in violation of the 50% facility time limits allowed in the manufacturing facility for the total requirements for the production of A101, A102, and A105. The lead times for component delivery make it impossible to obtain monthly schedules for every component for every month of the year. However, an MRP schedule should be obtained for each component for as many months into the current year as can be done, given the existing forecasts for A1 and A2, without trying to project the forecasts of A1 and A2 any farther out in time.

Freda Metal Furniture Co.

Freda Metal Furniture Company (FMFC) produces a wide range of metal furniture for a number of different uses. One of their specialty areas centers on the production of high-quality metal office furniture. The FMFC facility that produces steel office desks wants to establish a Material Requirements Plan (MRP) system to schedule the production of all components for these desks. Two specific products, of the many products produced at this facility, have been identified for use as a trial case for an MRP model. The two products are their Full Desk unit and their Work Station unit, since these two products have many components in common.

Exhibits 16.1 and 16.2 show a diagram of the different levels of component production for Full Desk units and Work Station units respectively. Using Exhibit 16.1 as a basis, we expand on the process of producing a Full Desk unit (FD). Each FD is produced in a final assembly operation from five different components:

- RLSP—A package that contains the right- and left-hand sides of the finished desk. This is purchased from an outside supplier on a fixed-order-quantity basis.
- TOP—The top writing surface of the desk, which is obtained from an outside supplier in a lot-for-lot (L4L) ordering process. FMFC applies a heavy-gauge surface

EXHIBIT 16.1   **Assembly Diagram for FMFC Full Desk Unit**

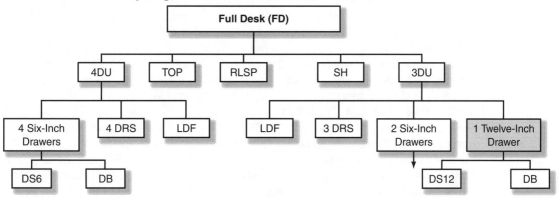

Note: The presence of an (↓) under any component indicates that the product structure that leads to that component is defined elsewhere.

EXHIBIT 16.2   **Assembly Diagram for FMFC Work Station Unit**

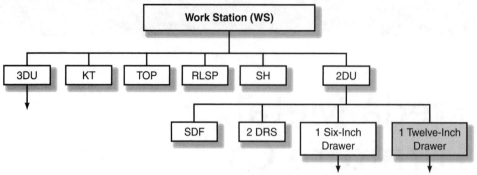

Note: The presence of an (↓) under any component indicates that the product structure that leads to that component is defined elsewhere.

of different color schemes to this writing surface just before it is sent to this assembly step.

- 4DU—This is a previously assembled component that is a frame that completely holds four drawers that are six inches in height. It is mounted underneath the top, on the left-hand side of the desk.
- 3DU—This is a previously assembled component that is a frame that completely holds three drawers. Two of these drawers are 6 inches in height and one of the drawers is 12 inches in height. It is mounted underneath the top, on the right-hand side of the desk.
- SH—This is a metal covering shield that spans the back of the desk to cover the gap between the 3DU and 4DU units, and it is purchased from an outside supplier in fixed-order quantities.

Workers put the components together with a combination of bolting and welding procedures that complete this process very quickly. All metal components are spray painted to the same color, and dried, in a very efficient process immediately before the final assembly takes place.

The drawer units, 4DU and 3DU, are assembled in an earlier operation, and they are then stored until they are used in the final assembly step. Each unit starts with a Large Drawer Frame (LDF) that is produced L4L in another FMFC facility at very high rates of output. One pair of sliding devices from a Drawer Roller Set (DRS) is attached to the inside of the LDF for each drawer that will be installed. That is, three DRS units are attached for a 3DU and four DRS units are attached for a 4DU. The DRS units support the drawers in the final assembly and allow for the easy opening and closing of the drawers in the finished product. The DRS units are attached to the LDF at appropriate heights that vary, depending upon whether a 3DU or a 4DU is being produced. Then all appropriate drawers are attached to their DRS units. The drawers that are used to produce 3DU and 4DU units are all assembled in a nearby facility as part of this operation on a L4L basis, and they are used immediately in the assembly of 3DU and 4DU units. The operation is performed in this fashion because of the extreme difficulty that would be encountered in stacking and storing assembled drawers that are not contained in an LDF.

All drawers are built with a process that starts with a package that contains an unassembled set of most of the subcomponents that are required to make a drawer. This package contains the front, back, and two sides of the drawer, and it is denoted as DS12 for a 12-inch drawer and DS6 for a 6-inch drawer. A common drawer bottom (DB) is added to the components from DS12 or DS6 to produce the finished drawer. This added DB unit is identical for all drawers. The DS12 and DS6 are obtained from a different division of FMFC. They are produced very quickly once their production process is set up, and they are ordered on a L4L basis. The DB units are very simple metal components, and they are purchased from an outside vendor in fixed-order quantities.

The Work Station unit (WS) is produced in a similar fashion with many of the same components as the FD unit, as shown in Exhibit 16.2. The 4DU unit in the FD is replaced by a Two Drawer unit (2DU), which holds one drawer that is 6 inches in height and one drawer that is 12 inches in height. The 2DU unit is produced in the same way as 4DU and 3DU units, except that the two drawers are contained inside a Small Drawer Frame (SDF) instead of an LDF. The WS unit also has a Keyboard Tray (KT) that attaches beneath the top and slides out when the WS is being used. KT is purchased from an outside supplier in fixed-order quantities.

Forecasted monthly demand values for both FD and WS units for the next year are shown in Exhibit 16.3. Different ordering procedures are used for different components in order to meet the demand schedule in Exhibit 16.3. L4L ordering is used for some of the components, and various appropriate Economic Order Quantity (EOQ) models are used for all other components, including FD and WS. Items that use L4L as a lot-sizing rule are denoted with L4L as the setup cost in Exhibit 16.4. All relevant costs for obtaining order quantities are given in Exhibit 16.4, along with the associated lead times, in months, and the existing inventory on hand for each of the components. The holding cost estimates in Exhibit 16.4 represent the annual variable holding cost for each associated component. As a general rule, FMFC assesses annual variable holding costs at 18% of the value of all costs that are associated with the components.

All fixed-order-quantity values should be rounded up or down to the nearest multiple of 100 units for convenience in placing and processing orders. The holding cost entry for DRS in Exhibit 16.4 is missing. At present, FMFC can order these units in any quantity from an outside supplier at a price of $2.50 per DRS unit. The supplier has just offered FMFC a 6% discount if they will order in shipments of 40,000 units per order or more. All order quantities for components should be determined on the basis of total actual annual demand from the forecasted demand for the final products, not on the basis of the number of units that will be produced during the next year. Once existing

EXHIBIT 16.3	Month	FD	WS	Month	FD	WS
Forecasted	1	2,000	900	7	1,600	800
Monthly	2	1,500	800	8	1,700	600
Demand	3	3,000	1,400	9	2,500	1,100
Values for	4	2,000	1,200	10	1,800	800
FD and WS	5	1,800	800	11	2,500	1,200
	6	2,500	1,000	12	2,000	900

EXHIBIT 16.4 **Ordering and Lot Sizing Information for FD and WS Components**

Component	Source	On Hand	Lead Time	Setup Cost	Holding Cost
FD	Assembly	3,000	1	$14,500	$80.20
WS	Assembly	1,900	1	$7,550	$77.00
RLSP	Purchase	6,000	1	$1,855	$5.40
TOP	Purchase	8,000	2	L4L	—
KT	Purchase	2,000	2	$490	$2.80
SH	Purchase	5,000	1	$1,535	$3.10
4DU	Assembly	6,000	2	$3,450·	$22.95
3DU	Assembly	8,000	2	$7,900	$18.25
2DU	Assembly	2,500	2	$4,200	$17.05
LDF	Produce	9,000	1	L4L	
SDF	Produce	3,500	1	L4L	
DRS	Purchase	30,000	1	$875	—
DS6	Purchase	23,000	1	L4L	
DS12	Purchase	9,000	1	L4L	
DB	Purchase	30,000	1	$370	$0.14

inventories are used up, ordering will continue on an ongoing basis, and the ongoing order quantities will be driven by total actual demand.

All orders from outside suppliers will come to FMFC in single shipments. Almost all assembly and production operations within FMFC, including the final assembly of FD and WS units, operate so quickly that the shipments effectively arrive in instantaneous receipt once a run is started. However, the facility that produces 2DU, 3DU, and 4DU units is much more labor intense than the other operations. The 2DU, 3DU, and 4DU units are assembled at a rate of 2,500 units/week, 6,000 units/week, and 3,000 units/week, respectively, at a FMFC department that produces many other components for FMFC divisions. These units cannot be produced concurrently, and the units are added to FMFC inventory as they are produced. FMFC operates 48 weeks per year, with approximately four workweeks in each month during the year, and components are only withdrawn from inventory for use during these weeks. Production of the units takes place during the first month of the lead time. The units are inspected, painted, and shipped during the second month of the lead time.

FMFC management wants to see an MRP schedule for FD and WS, along with all of their components, to meet the forecasted demand schedule for the next year. In order to account for the possibility of forecast error, the expected ending inventory of each of FD and WS in each month should be at least 25% of their respective forecasted demand for the following month. Order receipt quantities should not be predicted at any time for any unit in the MRP schedule. That is, no order receipt entries should be made for any component in any month of the MRP schedule unless the precise requirements for that component can be determined.

Once the MRP has been established, it must be checked to account for an additional problem. The facility that produces the 2DU, 3DU, and 4DU units has many other demands placed on it for other activities. As a result, they can never allow more than 50%

of the available time in any work month to producing these three units. This limitation applies only during the first month of the lead time for 2DU, 3DU, and 4DU, when the units are being produced. If the MRP violates this capacity restriction, it must be modified so that this capacity restriction is not violated. If a component is shifted back to a previous month in which it is already being processed, the two runs can be made consecutively in the previous month to avoid the setup cost for the second run in the sequence. It is not practical to consider moving any run back more than one month. FMFC has a strict policy that prohibits the use of overtime to meet any needs for extra capacity.

Peaquad Apparel Company

The Peaquad Apparel Company (PAC) produces upscale clothing that is sold at numerous vacation venues. Most of their business is done with major beach resorts in the summer and ski areas in the winter. Their business with retail outlets at any given beach area is typically for high quality T-shirts that have the name of the beach area printed or embroidered onto the shirt. Similarly, their business with retail outlets at ski areas usually consists of sweatshirts, pullovers, and sweaters that have the name of the given ski resort printed or embroidered onto them. PAC is a well-established business with a solid customer base, and their business has been very successful in recent years.

PAC management is considering the possibility of making some changes in their supply chain operation that could significantly reduce their total inventory holding cost while maintaining a high inventory service level. Of course, this change will require some initial expenditure, and PAC management wants to see some formal analysis to determine if the initial expense that would be required would be offset by the associated reduction in total inventory holding cost within some reasonable time frame.

THE EXISTING SITUATION

Attention will be initially restricted to the part of PAC's business that deals with supplying T-shirts to beach areas in order to consider how the problem might be analyzed. Since PAC deals in high-quality merchandise, they produce their own T-shirts from material that they purchase from suppliers in order to be assured of meeting the quality specifications they require. The shirts are then dyed to some background color if necessary, and some lines of shirts go through a tie-dye process in this stage. After the shirts have dried, all base designs are then put on the shirts with a screening process. This base design includes all of the artwork and writing on the shirt beyond the background color, excluding the name of a specific beach resort area. The same basic shirts are supplied to most beach areas, and the names of the specific beach areas are added to the shirts in a final step before they are shipped to distributors. The process for making shirts, dyeing them, and adding basic designs requires a rather sophisticated process with the high volume of shirts that PAC deals in. The process of adding the name of a specific beach to the shirt in the final step is a very simple procedure.

The main PAC production facility keeps an inventory of each of the basic types of shirts in their product line. All orders are sent to the main production facility from local distributors that are all part of PAC's operation, so that a cost reduction for distributors is a cost reduction for PAC. Each distributor has an assigned geographic district, and they can sell PAC products to all of the retail outlets around all of the beach resort areas within their assigned district. Each distributor has sales personnel who make weekly calls on the retail outlets to take orders and then make arrangements for deliveries a few days later from the inventory maintained at the distribution center. Weekly demand for this product is highly dependent on weather, particularly on weather over weekends, so there is a dramatic variability in demand.

Retail outlets at most beach resorts obviously generate almost all of their revenue during the summer months, so it is unacceptable to the retailers for distributors to have frequent inventory stockouts during these crucial months for their business. The receipt of orders from the distributor within a few days of order placement is critical to the successful operation of the retail outlets. There is a two-week lead time for orders to be received by the distributor after an order is placed with the production facility. Much of this lead time results from the amount of time needed to ship the shirts. As a result, each distributor maintains an inventory of shirts for each beach area in its district. Close control is maintained over inventory at the distribution centers, with orders being placed according to a perpetual, or fixed-order-quantity, system.

PAC distributors have been carrying safety stock for each style of shirt in their product line that will give a 99% service level for the retailers in each beach area for that particular style of shirt. That is, distributors carry an inventory of each style of shirt for each beach area so that there is a 99% chance that no stockouts will occur for each particular style of shirt in each individual beach area during the distributor's order cycle. As a result, each PAC distributor carries a very large accumulated volume of safety stock throughout the summer. Moreover, with the number of different shirt styles in PAC's product line and the number of beach areas that are covered by each distributor, the overall service level for each distributor across all shirt styles and beach areas falls drastically below the 99% target.

THE PROPOSED SUPPLY CHAIN MODIFICATION

The proposed change to the supply chain operation that was mentioned above would have the production facility shipping shirts to the distribution centers without the name of any beach area on them. Since the process of adding names is very simple and it can be done very quickly, this would not reduce the existing two-week lead time for the production facility to deliver orders to distributors. The necessary equipment would be provided to distributors so that they could add the names of beach areas to the shirts as orders are being filled. The sales force for a distributor would take orders as before and report back to the distributor. The beach area names would then be added to the ordered shirts as specified in the orders from retailers on an overnight basis, and the shirts would still be ready for delivery in a few days, as the current system operates.

Some training that is related to the operation of the new equipment would have to be provided at the distribution centers, but the procedure is quite simple. The cost of labor that would be required to perform the new operation at the distribution centers would be directly offset by the fact that the operation would no longer have to be performed at the main production facility. The cost of installing the new equipment at a distribution center could be offset by the reduction in the total cost for holding inventory at the distribution centers.

With this new system, distributors only have to maintain inventory for each line of shirt, without having to maintain individual quantities of inventory for each line of shirt that is specified for each beach area. Since the accumulated annual orders for each line of shirts from the production facility is unchanged in both scenarios, there will be no change in their inventory policies or in the annual costs for holding basic inventory to meet expected demand. However, there should be significant reductions in the costs that are associated with carrying safety stock under the modified procedure.

PAC management wants to see some analysis to determine the reduction in annual cost that can be expected if the new system is implemented. They are obtaining cost estimates for buying and setting up the necessary equipment for each distributor. Their ultimate interest is in determining how long it will take to pay for the associated investment with the cost savings that can be expected.

THE TYPICAL PATTERN OF WEEKLY DEMAND

Some data was collected for a typical distribution center to facilitate the analysis of this problem. The territory that has been laid out for each distribution center was determined so that each has about the same sales potential, so each should have roughly the same patterns of demand. The specific distribution center that was selected includes 10 major beach areas: Ishmael (B1), Ahab (B2), Moby (B3), Melville (B4), Birches (B5), Students (B6), Toothaker (B7), Dollar (B8), Sandy (B9), and Bugle (B10).

Exhibit 17.1 shows the weekly demand for one of the leading lines of PAC shirts at each of these 10 beach areas for the most recent summer season. As mentioned above, there is a lot of variability in weekly demand that is accounted for mostly by weather conditions. These beaches are far enough apart that their weekly demand values can be assumed to be independent of the demand at other beaches. Special orders and custom designed shirts will continue to be handled by the existing procedure.

The demand patterns in Exhibit 17.1 are typical of what should be expected. Week 1 is the last week in May, which accounts for Memorial Day with the traditional start of the busy season at the beaches in this district. The distributor does not carry any inventory of these T-shirts during the off-season. Before the start of the busy season, orders are taken from retailers in the beach areas and the distributor places a large order with the production facility. This initial order will be adequate to stock the retail outlets, to establish the basic inventory for the distributor to meet expected demand, and to establish any required safety stock for inventory. So, safety stock will start being carried

EXHIBIT 17.1 Weekly Demand for T-Shirts for the Selected PAC Distributor

Week	B1	B2	B3	B4	B5	B6	B7	B8	B9	B10
1	1,046	1,511	1,137	1,289	2,273	1,859	1,599	1,012	566	1,310
2	1,030	817	985	2,132	1,741	671	2,448	653	1,114	902
3	1,027	524	1,239	1,966	2,018	1,468	1,365	648	1,476	774
4	515	626	908	1,676	1,684	1,086	2,404	1,311	841	1,082
5	1,035	1,065	960	1,768	1,944	1,223	1,699	1,151	1,135	1,492
6	981	1,492	1,171	1,366	1,521	1,606	2,591	1,252	1,050	813
7	389	1,508	601	1,949	2,239	1,918	1,936	1,490	751	1,412
8	756	1,773	771	1,135	1,253	1,521	1,167	1,793	1,225	978
9	1,152	738	901	1,870	949	675	1,890	1,463	686	1,068
10	511	1,671	1,140	999	1,917	1,296	1,349	436	1,251	1,360
11	449	1,331	638	1,884	1,772	1,389	1,724	1,366	1,207	1,126
12	1,079	1,423	1,091	1,225	2,165	1,776	1,702	1,254	1,108	1,432
13	987	1,209	915	897	1,902	1,554	1,509	1,119	897	907
14	329	1,075	723	1,012	1,500	981	898	1,118	592	1,559
15	1,368	1,655	1,470	1,928	2,327	2,201	1,822	1,625	1,647	1,865

during Week 1 of the annual cycle, and business will continue normally during the 13 weeks in June, July, and August.

The very high demand values for Week 15 represent an aberration in the data that is presented in Exhibit 17.1 since it corresponds to Labor Day weekend during the first week in September. This marks the end of the main summer season for the beaches in the distribution area in question. Final orders for the season are supplied to retail outlets for this week, and the retail outlets that continue to stay open will deal with the remaining significantly decreased weekly demand over the rest of the season with the inventory that they have left at the end of this week. The distributor takes orders from retailers for Week 15 two weeks in advance and places orders with the production facility so that the retail orders will be met, while clearing out all remaining inventory that the distributor is holding. As a result, the distributor does not expect to be carrying any inventory during Week 15, so that inventory is only carried from Week 1 through Week 14.

THE DESIRED ANALYSIS

PAC management wants two basic pieces of information that are related to making the proposed change in the existing supply chain operation. With the change, PAC would be holding safety stock to maintain a 99% service level for each style of shirt for each distributor, which is expected to be an improvement over the existing situation. A reasonable estimate is desired for the actual overall service level that the distributor currently has for the selected style of shirt from Exhibit 17.1 with the existing supply chain policy. This will provide PAC management with some idea of the impact that the proposed change will have on their overall service levels.

The second issue is based on a desired cost analysis. The only impact that the proposed change will have on expected annual inventory costs is on the holding cost for safety stock. PAC assesses their variable cost to hold any item in inventory for an entire year at 15% of their total investment in a given item. The style of shirt that is considered in the data in Exhibit 17.1 has a total investment of $10.40 for PAC. The marginal investment for PAC to add a beach area name to a shirt can be considered to be insignificant, since that the cost of acquiring the associated equipment that is needed to perform the activity would be a fixed cost.

The line of shirts in Exhibit 17.1 is a major component of the associated distributor's sales of non-customized shirts. It accounts for 16% of these sales by the given distributor, and all lines of shirts have costs that are roughly the same. PAC management wants an estimate of the expected annual-cost savings from reduced safety stock that would result from implementing the proposed change with the selected distributor.

Nemo Power Supply

Nemo Power Supply (NPS) is a company that manufactures and distributes power supply units for many different electrical products. These units transform AC current from standard electric outlets to DC current that is used as the power source for many electrical devices. Common applications of NPS products are for use to power laptop computers and to power units that recharge cellular telephones. All of the product lines of power supply units that NPS manufactures use the same basic technology. Any differences account for the desired voltage of the DC power that is to be supplied as output and for differing characteristics of AC power that can be used as input.

NPS was originally founded many years ago in Dallas, where the company's only production facility exists. Over the years, 12 regional distribution centers have been established for NPS products throughout the United States: Seattle (L1), San Francisco (L2), San Diego (L3), Dallas (L4), Kansas City (L5), Minneapolis (L6), Chicago (L7), New Orleans (L8), Boston (L9), New York (L10), Atlanta (L11), and Miami (L12). The company is very content with this network of distribution sites, since it allows for close contact with NPS customers. On-time delivery and the maintenance of sufficient inventory to ensure high service levels are critical to the strong customer base that NPS has developed. NPS management has established a 99.5% target service level rate for all items that they keep in inventory. That is, they want to maintain inventory at a level such that there is a 99.5% chance that there will not be any stockouts for each given product during its order cycle.

Each distribution center is currently working with about as many customers in their respective regions as they can comfortably deal with, while maintaining the required degree of customer rapport that is essential to the business. Currently NPS management has no issues of concern related to this network of distribution locations. However, there are serious concerns over the production facility. The facility in Dallas is nearing the end of its expected useful life. Without a major overhaul of this facility, quality control issues and excessive maintenance costs can be expected to develop. The cost estimates for such an overhaul are very high, which has led to the conclusion that it might be time to consider building a new facility in a different location. This is particularly true since the relative location of the Dallas facility in the existing web of distribution centers that has evolved over time puts it at a significant disadvantage when considering the cost of shipping from the production facility to the distribution centers. The huge volume of units shipped from the production facility makes the cost of shipping a significant factor in the company's total cost of operation.

THE CENTRALIZED LOCATION OPTION

It would obviously cost more to build an entirely new production facility at a more centrally located site than to completely overhaul the existing facility in Dallas. However, the associated one-time additional expense might be worthwhile if NPS can offset this cost over some reasonable period of time with reduced shipping costs. In order to start their analysis of this option, NPS management wants to know where a new production facility should be located to minimize the total shipping cost to the 12 distribution centers. It is also of interest to have an estimate of the annual cost savings that would result from reduced shipping by building a new facility at the given location.

All shipping from the production center to the distribution centers is done by common carrier, and shipping costs for any unit can be assumed to be proportional to the straight-line distance between the shipping origin and the destination. In order to give some basis to the relative position of all of the distribution locations, a grid was drawn on a map, and grid coordinates were measured to scale for each distribution center in units of miles. The grid coordinates are listed in Exhibit 18.1 with the X-Coordinate entry referring to the relative East-West position and the Y-Coordinate referring to the relative North-South position for each distribution center.

While the information in Exhibit 18.1 can give an idea of the relative distances between the distribution centers, the number of units that are shipped to each distributor must be known in order to evaluate the total shipping cost from any specified location for a production facility.

A representative product, PS-4, was selected to aid in this analysis. The demand for PS-4s is typical of the relative demand patterns for all NPS products at each distribution center. Unit shipping costs to any given location from a specified production site will be about the same for all NPS products, and the PS-4 constitutes about 10% of the total number of units that are produced and shipped annually. Records were evaluated to determine the total weekly demand for PS-4s at each of the 12 distribution centers for the past 26 weeks. The results are summarized in Exhibit 18.2, and the accumulated demands from the 26-week interval can be doubled to obtain reasonable annual demand estimates for each distributor.

EXHIBIT 18.1
Grid
Coordinates
for NPS
Distribution
Centers

Distributor	X-Coordinate	Y-Coordinate
L1	300	1,950
L2	225	1,350
L3	270	750
L4	1,050	525
L5	900	975
L6	1,200	1,425
L7	1,800	1,200
L8	2,100	750
L9	2,700	1,500
L10	2,550	1,275
L11	2,400	450
L12	2,625	150

EXHIBIT 18.2   Demand for PS–4 Units at each NPS Distributor

Week	L1	L2	L3	L4	L5	L6	L7	L8	L9	L10	L11	L12
1	12,673	9,527	9,675	10,563	9,009	7,252	8,685	6,976	12,543	10,217	7,557	5,549
2	15,761	11,849	12,033	13,138	11,205	9,019	8,115	6,519	11,721	9,548	7,062	5,185
3	14,856	11,169	11,343	12,384	10,562	8,501	8,814	7,080	12,730	10,370	7,670	5,632
4	16,091	12,098	12,286	13,413	11,440	9,208	9,094	7,304	13,134	10,699	7,913	5,810
5	12,005	9,026	9,166	10,007	8,535	6,870	9,270	7,446	13,388	10,906	8,067	5,923
6	16,006	12,034	12,221	13,342	11,379	9,160	8,282	6,652	11,961	9,743	7,207	5,291
7	14,101	10,601	10,766	11,754	10,025	8,069	6,990	5,614	10,095	8,223	6,082	4,466
8	10,343	7,776	7,897	8,622	7,353	5,919	10,662	8,564	15,398	12,543	9,278	6,812
9	11,216	8,432	8,563	9,349	7,974	6,418	8,926	7,169	12,891	10,501	7,767	5,703
10	15,127	11,373	11,549	12,609	10,754	8,656	7,836	6,294	11,318	9,219	6,819	5,007
11	11,714	8,807	8,944	9,764	8,328	6,703	11,685	9,386	16,875	13,747	10,168	7,466
12	11,597	8,719	8,854	9,667	8,245	6,636	9,240	7,422	13,345	10,871	8,041	5,904
13	13,624	10,243	10,402	11,357	9,686	7,811	8,710	6,996	12,580	10,247	7,579	5,565
14	13,735	10,326	10,486	11,449	9,765	7,860	7,245	5,819	10,463	8,535	6,304	4,629
15	13,127	9,869	10,022	10,942	9,332	7,512	11,460	9,205	16,551	13,483	9,973	7,322
16	14,203	10,678	10,844	11,839	10,097	8,127	10,478	8,417	15,133	12,328	9,118	6,695
17	11,055	8,312	8,454	9,215	7,860	6,326	13,272	10,660	19,181	15,614	11,549	8,480
18	14,920	11,217	11,392	12,437	10,607	8,538	9,585	7,689	13,825	11,262	8,330	6,116
19	11,999	9,021	9,161	10,002	8,531	6,867	10,841	8,708	15,657	12,754	9,433	6,926
20	11,223	8,437	8,568	9,355	7,979	6,422	7,989	6,417	11,538	9,399	6,952	5,118
21	13,223	9,941	10,096	11,022	9,401	7,567	8,443	6,781	12,193	9,933	7,347	5,394
22	10,153	7,633	7,752	8,478	7,218	5,810	9,673	7,784	13,970	11,380	8,429	6,180
23	15,327	11,537	11,702	12,776	10,897	8,771	10,656	8,559	15,389	12,536	9,272	6,808
24	11,322	8,512	8,644	9,438	8,049	6,479	11,453	9,200	16,541	13,475	9,966	7,318
25	16,322	12,271	12,462	13,606	11,617	9,340	7,787	6,255	11,247	9,162	6,776	4,975
26	10,777	8,092	8,218	8,972	7,652	6,159	11,309	9,084	16,333	13,305	9,841	7,226

Records indicate that a total of $305,000 was spent to ship all of the PS-4s to distributors during the given 26-week interval, with all units being shipped from the production facility in Dallas (L4). Any future growth in demand should increase with a consistent percentage rate for all distributors.

THE SPLIT FACILITY OPTION

One of the NPS managers has suggested another option, which involves establishing two different production facilities, instead of one. The 12 distribution centers can easily be divided into two groups. L1 through L6 are concentrated in the western half of the country while L7 through L12 are concentrated in the eastern half of the country. The Western Division and the Eastern Division both have most of their distribution centers located near their respective coasts. As a result, any centrally located production facility must incur very high shipping costs. In addition, the total annual demand for distributors in the Western Division is about the same as the total annual demand for distributors in the Eastern Division with this classification of distributors.

It is quite evident that the establishment of separate production facilities for both divisions would have a dramatic impact on the reduction of total shipping costs, since each can be located to minimize the cost of shipping to the distributors within their respective divisions. There will be an increased total cost involved with the initial construction of two separate production facilities with the "Split Facility Option" when it is compared to total construction cost of the "Centralized Location Option." As before, the associated reduction in total shipping cost with the Split Facility Option might offset this one-time incremental cost of implementation over some reasonable period of time.

NPS management wants to know where the two production facilities would be located with the Split Facility Option in order to minimize total shipping cost, along with an estimate of what the associated total annual shipping cost would be. If the Split Facility Option is implemented, cross shipping between the Eastern and Western Divisions will be strongly discouraged, in order to maintain the "ownership" and control that the individual production facilities will have within their divisions.

Another NPS manager has raised some additional issues that must be considered with the Split Facility Option. These issues are all related to the associated operating costs, beyond shipping costs, for having two production facilities instead of one. The additional operating costs include the cost for production run setups, the cost for carrying basic inventory, and the cost of carrying sufficient safety stock to maintain the 99.5% service level on a company-wide basis for all product lines. The necessity of maintaining this high service level is not a policy that anyone questions. It would seem that all of these costs would be different under the two options.

The process used to produce power supply units is such that it operates most efficiently by producing large runs of given units between changeovers. The inventory from these large runs is stored at the production facility, with shipments being made to the distribution centers on a regular basis. This allows for the holding of relatively small inventories at the individual distribution centers, while still avoiding the possibility of stockouts, since customers usually do not require immediate deliveries. Stockouts will occur only if the production facility runs out of inventory. Inventory at the production facility is monitored very closely on an ongoing basis, so that a perpetual, or fixed-order-quantity, system is used to trigger production runs.

The analysis of all of the operating costs that have been mentioned for the two options can be continued with the PS-4 data. The variable component of annual holding cost for PS-4 is $10.25/unit, which is comparable to the holding cost of all NPS products. The single production facility with the Centralized Location Option would have an output rate of 1,200,000 units/week for PS-4, once the system is set up for a production run. The setup cost for a production run is very high, since this is a very sophisticated system. The setup also involves extensive preliminary quality control testing in the initial stages before a full production run. This preliminary testing provides assurance that the system is working properly before full-scale production is initiated. Unfortunately, this preliminary testing requires the ultimate destruction of a large number of the power supply units. The net result is that the total cost of setting up for a production run of PS-4 units is $90,000/setup. The Split Facility Option will have two facilities, each of which has an output rate of 600,000 units/week and a setup cost of $45,000/setup. There will be a two-week lead-time for a production run under both options.

An additional problem associated with this decision relates to the variation in demand at the distribution centers. NPS sells power supply units to many different customers that use their power supply units in numerous end products. Some of these customers are competitors in the market for similar end products. Any of these customers can initiate a major marketing effort with price discounts for one of their end products at any time that they choose to do so. This will lead to an increase in their demand for the associated power supply units from NPS, with the likely impact of reducing their competitor's demand for the same type of power supply units from NPS. If these competitors are not both in the Eastern or Western Division, then both Divisions will have variations in their individual demand levels for this particular power supply unit, while the total demand for NPS experiences a much smaller variation.

Given that the Split Facility Option will strongly discourage cross shipping between the Eastern and Western Divisions, each production facility must hold sufficient inventory to meet a service level within their respective divisions so that the overall service level for NPS is 99.5%. Most of NPS's customers are not competitors, as described above. As a result, the service level that each production facility must maintain to meet the company-wide 99.5% service level can be reasonably approximated in this case by assuming that the demands in the Eastern and Western Divisions are independent. However, the production facilities in the Eastern and Western Divisions should both be using inventory policies with the same service level.

SUMMARY

NPS management wants to see estimates of the total annual expected operating cost for all of their products, not just for PS-4, for both the Centralized Location Option and the Split Facility Option. All of the costs that have been given for PS-4 units can be assumed to be about the same for all of the power supply units that NPS produces, and it was mentioned above that PS-4 accounts for about 10% of all business for NPS. These estimates of the annual expected operating cost for both options should be broken down for each of the relevant components of operating costs: shipping, setup, basic inventory holding, and the additional expected cost for holding safety stock. Other costs for such things as raw materials and labor can be ignored in this analysis, since they will be about the same under both options.

Once management has estimates of these total expected annual operating costs for both options, they can make a determination on financial grounds as to whether or not the additional one-time cost of building two production facilities can be recaptured in a reasonable amount of time.

Quality Control

Seattle Concrete Company

Seattle Concrete Company (SCC) has been in the business of producing concrete mix for many years. SCC produces bags of standard concrete premix that consumers typically buy at lumberyards or hardware stores for home improvement projects. The concrete mix is put into 40-pound bags that are shipped in large quantities to wholesale distributors.

A very simple process is used to produce the actual concrete mix, and SCC has absolutely no problems with its basic production process. However, a critical issue is to make certain that the correct number of pounds of the mix is placed in each of the bags. SCC would be subject to some potentially serious fines and penalties if random sampling, after sale, showed any significant shortage below the 40-pound fill that is specified on the bags. The process of filling bags is far from perfect, so some natural variation in the fill of each bag is to be expected. To avoid potential problems from this natural variability in fill, SCC has a targeted fill level of 41 pounds for each bag, so that a slight underfill from the target would still meet the 40-pound specification.

SCC uses statistical process control charts to monitor the operations at their facility. They have been operating on a single eight-hour shift basis, until recently, without any significant problems. A random sample of 10 bags has been taken and weighed once every hour during shift operations, with the results of the hourly sampling being noted and plotted on X-bar and R control charts, with all control chart limits being based upon 3-σ standards. After the hourly sampling is done, the shift supervisor is supposed to check the equipment that fills the bags, to verify that concrete mix is not building up in the series of chutes that deliver the mix to the bags. If the buildup of mix in the chutes becomes excessive, the end result is that there can tend to be a lot of variability in the fill of the bags. If a buildup has started to accumulate, it is a relatively quick and easy task to have someone remove the buildup by using a rake-like device to clear the chutes. The regular shift supervisor at SCC has been on the job for many years and is known to be a very diligent worker.

Due to a high increase in demand, SCC has recently added a second shift to the operation in order to significantly increase output. Totally different employees are used on the second shift. A high-seniority worker from the first shift was given additional training to become the shift supervisor for this new second-shift operation. SCC management wants to establish a procedure to monitor the operations across both shifts with statistical process control charts to be assured that there is consistency in output at all times.

Some information is required to get started on this procedure, so some preliminary data has been collected. Exhibit 19.1 shows sample weights from 40 different sampling events during the regular shift operation. These sampling events took place in each of the eight shift hours over five consecutive workdays in a week, during which the operation was running normally throughout the entire week. Following the discussion above, Exhibit 19.1 shows the recorded weights of the 10 bags that were selected during each specific sampling event. Random samples of 10 bags each have also been taken and weighed during each operating hour on the second shift, just like they have in the regular first-shift operation. The results of sampling from five days of the second shift operation are shown in Exhibit 19.2.

SCC management wants to see a statistical process control analysis performed for each of the shifts, showing the resulting X-bar and R control charts with 3-σ standards, over the 40 sampling events that took place during each of the shifts. Any information that can be provided about the consistency of output over the two shifts would be very helpful to SCC management.

EXHIBIT 19.1   Test Results from the First-Shift Sampling

Day	Hour	Observation									
		1	2	3	4	5	6	7	8	9	10
1	1	40.94	40.21	39.89	40.25	40.64	40.37	41.97	42.10	41.90	40.82
	2	42.32	40.55	40.77	42.30	41.25	40.63	41.21	39.96	40.68	41.34
	3	39.56	42.53	41.93	39.90	41.40	42.46	42.91	41.55	41.19	41.50
	4	39.89	40.20	41.33	39.31	39.46	40.31	41.56	41.16	41.37	41.57
	5	40.83	40.36	39.03	40.59	41.54	42.52	39.61	39.98	40.03	41.67
	6	39.41	41.68	40.85	41.69	40.10	42.25	40.68	41.13	38.51	41.91
	7	41.29	41.13	42.20	39.58	41.33	41.90	41.67	39.82	41.26	41.17
	8	40.89	39.90	41.22	39.67	41.18	39.69	41.05	42.97	42.17	39.23
2	1	40.94	41.94	38.98	41.59	42.51	41.58	39.76	41.56	38.92	41.30
	2	39.74	40.50	39.45	42.01	41.97	41.40	41.96	42.17	40.80	41.24
	3	39.83	40.57	41.40	39.32	41.12	40.13	38.13	41.95	40.67	40.65
	4	40.97	40.56	42.27	42.05	41.18	41.92	41.84	39.25	39.78	40.86
	5	40.46	43.17	42.43	41.72	39.99	40.98	41.24	41.39	41.52	42.17
	6	42.91	41.86	40.84	40.71	40.23	43.46	40.81	40.46	40.11	42.38
	7	40.72	42.11	41.52	40.02	41.55	40.11	40.86	40.63	40.02	41.68
	8	41.67	40.77	39.42	42.18	39.65	39.79	42.37	38.84	41.05	41.30
3	1	39.98	42.91	40.74	41.98	40.32	41.05	41.62	40.33	40.85	40.76
	2	41.84	41.70	40.84	40.38	41.08	42.07	42.72	38.77	41.13	40.74
	3	42.69	42.21	40.19	42.27	41.06	42.33	39.90	42.11	40.10	40.30
	4	41.45	42.22	41.46	38.82	41.67	39.69	41.72	42.53	43.27	40.91
	5	40.35	40.10	41.65	39.77	43.18	41.22	40.29	39.89	40.28	41.31
	6	41.28	41.43	43.75	41.74	40.61	42.02	39.34	40.14	41.12	39.20
	7	42.23	40.52	41.72	39.59	40.34	39.37	41.44	43.49	40.81	39.83
	8	40.53	42.31	42.71	42.86	43.17	41.42	42.58	40.18	40.87	40.45
4	1	41.48	42.03	40.80	40.81	39.67	40.53	42.05	41.27	41.40	41.98
	2	39.82	41.76	41.47	40.55	39.98	41.98	41.58	39.13	41.73	39.82
	3	40.18	41.21	42.63	42.51	39.99	39.89	40.31	41.09	39.89	40.15
	4	39.83	40.56	40.07	41.25	40.54	39.03	40.25	41.04	42.14	40.65
	5	41.87	41.87	42.04	41.18	41.27	40.26	40.89	40.70	42.37	40.07
	6	42.29	40.77	40.31	40.51	40.90	39.25	40.45	41.67	40.59	40.83
	7	43.23	42.84	40.14	41.49	40.51	39.51	42.32	41.96	41.38	40.56
	8	42.14	40.46	41.44	40.91	41.90	41.00	41.14	41.81	42.43	41.11
5	1	41.44	41.48	41.71	41.75	39.67	39.21	41.26	39.30	40.60	42.03
	2	41.41	41.01	41.97	40.35	40.16	39.45	40.55	41.16	40.29	42.49
	3	40.86	40.91	38.89	40.20	41.76	41.11	41.67	40.31	41.54	41.35
	4	40.17	41.91	41.51	40.45	43.01	40.18	40.67	41.79	39.86	40.68
	5	41.26	40.45	40.73	40.98	41.07	42.18	43.42	41.66	40.26	40.62
	6	41.33	37.68	40.70	40.88	40.56	40.90	41.64	40.98	39.67	39.23
	7	40.66	41.28	40.09	41.57	40.83	39.85	40.85	40.31	42.17	40.35
	8	41.19	41.37	39.55	40.97	42.22	41.03	42.42	41.26	40.50	40.35

EXHIBIT 19.2 **Test Results from the Second-Shift Sampling**

Day	Hour	Observation									
		1	2	3	4	5	6	7	8	9	10
1	1	40.94	40.21	40.64	40.25	40.64	40.37	42.30	41.35	41.90	40.82
	2	41.82	40.55	40.77	42.40	41.25	40.63	41.21	40.06	40.68	41.34
	3	39.91	42.53	41.93	39.99	41.40	42.46	42.66	41.55	41.19	41.50
	4	39.89	40.20	41.33	39.35	39.46	40.31	41.56	41.16	41.37	42.07
	5	40.83	40.36	39.03	40.59	41.54	42.52	39.61	39.98	40.03	41.67
	6	39.41	41.68	40.85	41.69	40.10	42.50	40.68	41.13	38.96	41.91
	7	41.29	41.13	42.70	39.08	41.33	41.90	41.67	39.82	41.26	41.17
	8	40.89	39.90	41.22	39.67	41.18	39.69	41.05	43.72	42.17	38.48
2	1	40.94	41.54	40.01	41.59	41.76	41.58	40.43	41.56	40.51	41.30
	2	40.13	40.50	39.95	42.01	41.97	41.40	41.96	41.67	40.80	41.24
	3	39.83	40.57	41.40	39.32	41.12	41.13	40.21	41.70	40.67	40.65
	4	40.97	40.56	42.27	42.05	41.18	41.92	41.84	39.25	39.78	40.86
	5	40.46	43.17	42.43	41.72	39.99	40.98	41.24	41.39	41.52	42.17
	6	43.16	41.86	40.84	40.71	40.23	42.46	40.81	40.46	39.86	42.38
	7	40.72	43.11	41.52	39.52	41.55	40.11	40.86	40.63	40.02	41.68
	8	41.67	40.77	39.42	42.18	39.65	39.79	43.12	38.09	41.05	41.30
3	1	40.73	42.16	40.74	41.98	40.32	41.05	41.62	40.33	40.85	40.76
	2	41.84	41.70	40.84	40.38	41.08	42.07	42.22	40.17	41.13	40.74
	3	42.14	42.21	40.19	42.27	41.06	42.33	39.75	42.11	39.81	40.30
	4	41.45	42.22	41.46	39.32	41.67	39.69	41.72	42.53	42.27	40.91
	5	40.35	40.10	41.65	39.77	43.18	41.22	40.29	39.89	40.28	41.31
	6	41.28	41.43	42.50	41.74	40.61	42.02	39.34	40.14	41.12	38.95
	7	42.23	40.52	41.72	39.59	40.34	38.87	41.44	42.65	40.81	39.83
	8	40.53	42.31	42.71	42.86	44.65	41.42	42.58	39.43	40.87	40.45
4	1	41.48	42.03	40.80	40.81	40.42	40.53	41.30	41.27	41.40	41.98
	2	39.82	41.76	41.47	40.55	39.98	41.48	41.58	39.63	41.73	39.82
	3	40.18	41.21	42.38	42.01	39.99	40.14	40.31	41.09	39.94	40.15
	4	39.83	40.56	40.07	41.25	40.54	39.53	40.25	41.04	42.14	40.65
	5	41.87	41.87	42.04	41.18	41.27	40.26	40.89	40.70	42.37	39.57
	6	42.54	40.77	40.31	40.51	40.90	39.50	40.45	41.67	40.59	40.83
	7	43.73	42.84	40.14	41.49	40.51	39.01	42.32	41.96	41.38	40.56
	8	38.41	40.46	41.44	40.91	41.90	40.50	37.65	41.81	42.98	41.11
5	1	41.44	41.48	41.71	41.75	39.97	39.96	41.26	39.91	40.60	41.28
	2	41.41	41.01	41.97	40.35	40.16	39.95	40.55	41.16	40.29	41.99
	3	40.86	40.91	39.34	40.20	41.51	41.11	41.67	40.31	41.54	41.35
	4	40.17	41.91	41.51	40.45	42.51	40.18	40.67	41.79	39.86	40.68
	5	41.26	40.45	40.73	40.98	41.07	41.18	43.42	41.66	40.56	40.62
	6	41.33	38.83	40.70	40.88	40.56	40.90	42.02	40.98	39.67	39.23
	7	40.66	41.28	40.09	41.57	40.83	39.35	40.85	40.31	43.14	40.35
	8	41.19	41.37	38.80	40.97	42.22	41.03	44.12	41.26	40.50	40.35

Case Twenty

Crouse Fuse Company

Many different companies produce electrical items that require fuses. These fuses act as a safety precaution, to terminate the flow of electrical current to a product if an excessive current starts to flow through it. The fuse prevents the possibility that the excessive current will cause components to burn out inside the product. This excessive power flow can result from various malfunctions inside the product itself, or from problems with the power source.

Crouse Fuse Company (CFC) produces very large amounts of inexpensive fuses for a number of different customers. Manufacturers of strings of outdoor lights use one of its primary product lines. These particular fuses consist of high-resistance thin metallic wires that are mounted inside a small glass tube. The electricity in the circuit is run through the wire inside the protective glass tube, and the resulting heat from any excessive current flow will melt the fuse wire. Once the fuse wire melts, the current flow through the system stops immediately. The diameter of the fuse wire and the makeup of its metallic content determine the current level at which the fuse will "blow out." These particular fuses are produced in very large quantities for various customers.

CFC has been named as a co-defendant, along with a light manufacturer, in a recent lawsuit. The lawsuit resulted from claims that some strings of lights did not shut down when short circuits developed. This resulted in property damage from fires in the homes of several people who were using the light strings for exterior decoration. Needless to say, CFC is extremely concerned about quality control issues.

The management of CFC realizes that their products cannot be perfect. This is particularly true since the market will only pay a very low price for this commodity item. In addition, fuses must be destroyed in order to test them. The testing process runs an electrical current through the fuse, and the fuse can fail testing in two ways. First, it can blow out at too low a level of electric current. That is, for levels of current that would exist during normal usage. If the fuse does not blow out at too low a level of current, the current level is then increased to determine at what level the fuse does blow out, to be assured that this level of power is not too high to meet safety standards. To pass the test, a fuse must blow out within an acceptable range of current levels. Clearly, CFC cannot perform 100% inspection, or there would be no product left to sell.

CFC management wants to establish statistical process control practices to monitor their facility, to be assured that quality control standards are being maintained over all shifts. In order to do this, we need to determine the operating characteristics of the process under normal conditions. To meet this end, CFC carefully monitored one of the shifts at its fuse production facility for one week. During this week of careful monitoring, the system was watched closely to ensure that everything was operating under normal conditions. A random sample of 50 fuses was taken once every 30 minutes during the eight-hour work shifts for five days in one workweek. The 50 fuses were tested, and the number of defective fuses in each sample was noted.

The results of all of this sampling are summarized in Exhibit 20.1. For example, Sample 12 on Day 1 occurred six hours into the shift operation on that day, when 50 fuses were tested to find that 2 were defective. All testing at CFC is done by quality control specialists in a unit that is independent of the fuse production facility, and all quality control test results that are reported can be assumed to be completely accurate. The test results in Exhibit 20.1 also represent normal operating conditions for the fuse-making facility, with output representing quality levels deemed acceptable to CFC, given all of the relevant conditions, customer expectations, and associated costs.

The most critical factor in fuse quality is the metallic content and the diameter of the wire inside the fuse. All shift supervisors were made aware of this situation, given the difficulties CFC is facing. The wire-forming operation can be calibrated periodically to reset its operation to precise specifications for the particular fuses being processed. The wire-forming process tends to "drift" over relatively short time periods, as replaceable components start to wear. This drift is a natural part of the operation, and there is no feasible way to change it. The wire-forming process can be recalibrated by shift supervisors at any time they choose to do so. At this time, the replaceable components are replaced, and other adjustments are made. However, the entire system significantly slows down during the time that recalibration is being done. A natural solution is to have the shift supervisors perform the recalibration before the start of each shift, and then again during an employee break that occurs after the first four hours of work on each shift. It has been made very clear to the shift supervisors that this recalibration procedure is of the utmost importance.

CFC wants to use statistical process control charts to control their fuse production process, and the test results from the monitored week can be used as a basis for establishing control chart limits (95% confidence is required) for future use. CFC runs two work shifts per day, and different shift supervisors are in charge on each shift. Testing has now been performed for both operating shifts for the first week of normal operation after the monitored week, using testing procedures that are identical to the procedures that were used during the monitored week. Testing results from the first and second shifts are given, respectively, in Exhibit 20.2 and Exhibit 20.3.

CFC management wants to see statistical process control analysis applied to the data from their system. This analysis should be based on the proportion of defective units in a sample, and it should be done on the data from both shifts. Any resulting input regarding differences in observations between the two shifts would be very helpful to CFC management, particularly if the observations might be some impact on productivity.

EXHIBIT 20.1
Quality
Control
Results from
Operation
during the
Monitored
Week

Day	Sample	Number Defective	Day	Sample	Number Defective
1	1	0	3	9	0
1	2	1	3	10	2
1	3	0	3	11	2
1	4	2	3	12	0
1	5	2	3	13	0
1	6	1	3	14	1
1	7	2	3	15	1
1	8	2	3	16	3
1	9	0	4	1	0
1	10	0	4	2	1
1	11	0	4	3	2
1	12	2	4	4	2
1	13	0	4	5	0
1	14	1	4	6	1
1	15	3	4	7	1
1	16	2	4	8	2
2	1	0	4	9	1
2	2	0	4	10	1
2	3	1	4	11	1
2	4	0	4	12	2
2	5	3	4	13	2
2	6	2	4	14	0
2	7	2	4	15	3
2	8	3	4	16	2
2	9	1	5	1	0
2	10	1	5	2	0
2	11	2	5	3	2
2	12	0	5	4	0
2	13	0	5	5	1
2	14	1	5	6	2
2	15	1	5	7	3
2	16	2	5	8	3
3	1	0	5	9	0
3	2	1	5	10	0
3	3	0	5	11	0
3	4	0	5	12	2
3	5	3	5	13	1
3	6	1	5	14	1
3	7	1	5	15	3
3	8	2	5	16	1

EXHIBIT 20.2
Quality
Control
Test Results
from the
First Shift

Day	Sample	Number Defective	Day	Sample	Number Defective
1	1	0	3	9	0
1	2	1	3	10	1
1	3	0	3	11	2
1	4	0	3	12	2
1	5	1	3	13	0
1	6	1	3	14	2
1	7	0	3	15	2
1	8	2	3	16	2
1	9	0	4	1	0
1	10	0	4	2	2
1	11	0	4	3	1
1	12	0	4	4	2
1	13	1	4	5	0
1	14	0	4	6	1
1	15	2	4	7	1
1	16	3	4	8	3
2	1	0	4	9	0
2	2	0	4	10	0
2	3	1	4	11	1
2	4	1	4	12	0
2	5	1	4	13	1
2	6	1	4	14	3
2	7	3	4	15	1
2	8	0	4	16	2
2	9	0	5	1	0
2	10	1	5	2	1
2	11	1	5	3	0
2	12	2	5	4	0
2	13	1	5	5	0
2	14	1	5	6	1
2	15	3	5	7	2
2	16	2	5	8	3
3	1	0	5	9	0
3	2	2	5	10	1
3	3	1	5	11	2
3	4	1	5	12	0
3	5	1	5	13	2
3	6	2	5	14	1
3	7	3	5	15	3
3	8	2	5	16	2

EXHIBIT 20.3
Quality
Control
Test Results
from the
Second Shift

Day	Sample	Number Defective	Day	Sample	Number Defective
1	1	0	3	9	0
1	2	0	3	10	0
1	3	1	3	11	0
1	4	0	3	12	1
1	5	1	3	13	0
1	6	1	3	14	0
1	7	1	3	15	0
1	8	2	3	16	1
1	9	0	4	1	0
1	10	1	4	2	1
1	11	1	4	3	1
1	12	1	4	4	1
1	13	0	4	5	0
1	14	0	4	6	0
1	15	2	4	7	1
1	16	2	4	8	1
2	1	0	4	9	0
2	2	1	4	10	1
2	3	0	4	11	1
2	4	2	4	12	2
2	5	0	4	13	0
2	6	1	4	14	0
2	7	1	4	15	0
2	8	1	4	16	1
2	9	0	5	1	0
2	10	1	5	2	0
2	11	1	5	3	0
2	12	2	5	4	1
2	13	0	5	5	0
2	14	1	5	6	1
2	15	2	5	7	1
2	16	1	5	8	2
3	1	0	5	9	0
3	2	0	5	10	0
3	3	0	5	11	1
3	4	1	5	12	1
3	5	0	5	13	0
3	6	0	5	14	0
3	7	1	5	15	0
3	8	2	5	16	1

Part Five

Project Management

Chadwick Construction Co.

Chadwick Construction Company (CCC) is a very large firm that has been involved in the business of constructing homes for a number of years. CCC buys large tracts of land in suburban areas all over the country, and then it supervises all subcontractors during the building of single-family residences in developments on these properties once local governments and environmental agencies have approved all aspects of the subdivision. Since the start of its business, CCC has overseen the construction of many thousands of homes. CCC employs many different teams of subcontractors in each of the 12 different specialty fields required for constructing houses. These specialty areas are:

- Excavation (Exc): This includes all excavation for the basement and the digging of all trenches for water and sewer lines.
- Concrete (Con): This includes laying of drainpipe, pouring concrete for the basement and driveway, and laying of blocks for the basement walls.
- Sewer and Water (S&W): This includes running sewer and water lines from the street to the main hookups in the basement.
- Structure (Str): This includes installation of the living space floor over the basement; putting up studs for all walls, roof, and ceilings; putting on a rough exterior siding; placing a rough waterproof covering over the rough outside siding and roof; installing insulation; and insertion of all exterior windows and doors.
- Electric (Ele): This includes running the main power line to the house, installing the main circuit box, and running all wires for the fixtures.
- Rough Plumbing (RPl): This includes installation of all pipes and tubing inside the walls of the structure for all sewer and water fixtures.
- Walls and Cabinets (W&C): This includes application of drywall and placement of kitchen cabinets.
- Finish Plumbing (FPl): This includes placement of all plumbing fixtures and a hot water heating system.
- Roofing and Siding (R&S): This includes installation of the roofing material, rain gutters, and exterior siding over part of the house.

- Inside Finish (IF): This includes plastering, painting, carpeting, trim work, and other activities to complete the inside of the house.
- Brick Work (BW): This includes application of bricks to parts of the exterior of the house and some decorative work around the house.
- Outside Finish (OF): This includes grading the yard, planting a lawn, and other landscaping work.

There are restrictions on the order in which activities can be completed. Neither Concrete nor Sewer and Water can start until excavation is done. Structure can only start after Concrete is done. Sewer and Water must be done before Rough Plumbing begins. Structure must be done before Roofing and Siding, Electric, and Rough Plumbing. Rough Plumbing and Electric must both be done before Walls and Cabinets can begin. Roofing and Siding must be done before Brick Work, and Brick Work must be done before Outside Finish. Walls and Cabinets must be done before Finish Plumbing, and both Finish Plumbing and Roofing and Siding must be done before Inside Finish.

These homes do have some variation in their design, but the amount of work that is required from each subcontractor specialty group to complete a given activity is about the same for each house. However, there is some natural variation in activity times for the subcontractors for each given activity. This variability is accounted for by factors such as weather, the availability of needed materials and equipment, and some absenteeism due to illness and injury. Exhibits 21.1 and 21.2 show the times that were required by each of the subcontractors for all activities over the last 40 homes that were built by CCC.

Nothing unusual happened during these observations, and the times represent what would normally be expected. These activity completion times are expressed in units of workdays. Enough activity times are reported in Exhibits 21.1 and 21.2 so that good estimates of optimistic, most likely, and pessimistic completion times can be obtained for each activity. These time estimates should be used as a basis to obtain expected completion times and activity time variances for each activity.

PROJECT MANAGEMENT PROBLEMS

CCC has had a significant increase in demand in recent years, and the general manager is considering the option of making some changes in operating procedures. Currently, subcontractors are scheduled for work at different sites when they check into the construction headquarters for the associated development, after completing work at the latest home to which they were assigned. The project management procedure is haphazard, at best. Exhibits 21.1 and 21.2 also show the total completion times for the last 40 houses that were built by CCC. Due to a lack of control over the assignment of subcontractors to jobs and a lack of monitoring the subcontractor crew progress at work sites, these total completion times are likely to be more than should be expected. As a result, the general manager is considering the possibility of hiring a project manager. The project manager would be responsible for using the basic notions of project scheduling to develop a schedule for when subcontractors should be working on each house, and then to keep track of the progress of the subcontractors at the work sites.

EXHIBIT 21.1   Number of Working Days for Activity Completion for CCC

Home	Exc.	Con.	S&W	Str.	Ele.	W&C	RPI	FPI	R&S	IF	BW	OF	House Time
1	5.0	11.0	4.0	58.0	4.5	9.0	5.0	5.0	15.5	5.0	7.5	7.0	107.0
2	6.0	7.0	6.5	67.0	4.0	11.0	3.0	6.0	15.5	7.5	8.0	6.5	120.0
3	4.0	11.5	5.0	60.0	4.0	9.5	5.0	5.5	14.0	8.0	7.0	7.5	110.5
4	4.5	12.0	4.5	53.0	7.0	7.5	8.5	4.5	16.0	6.5	5.5	9.0	100.5
5	5.0	10.5	5.0	46.0	4.0	9.0	2.5	5.5	15.0	13.0	6.0	5.5	100.0
6	4.5	11.5	5.5	57.0	5.0	8.5	4.5	3.5	17.5	7.5	9.0	6.5	102.0
7	5.0	13.0	6.5	68.0	5.5	10.0	6.0	5.0	20.0	9.5	10.0	8.0	123.5
8	5.5	11.0	3.5	65.0	4.5	11.5	3.5	4.5	15.5	5.5	6.5	7.0	119.5
9	4.5	11.5	6.0	55.0	9.5	10.5	7.0	5.0	14.0	8.5	8.0	6.0	101.0
10	4.5	10.0	4.5	60.0	5.0	9.5	7.5	6.0	18.5	8.0	7.0	9.5	116.5
11	6.0	12.5	5.0	58.0	4.5	9.0	9.0	5.5	15.0	7.0	5.0	11.0	104.0
12	5.0	10.0	4.0	57.0	5.5	8.5	6.0	4.5	16.5	6.0	9.5	6.5	106.5
13	5.5	11.5	4.5	64.0	3.5	9.5	13.5	6.5	15.0	7.5	4.5	6.5	111.0
14	5.0	11.0	5.0	54.0	5.0	10.0	6.0	5.0	14.5	10.5	6.0	8.0	112.0
15	4.5	12.5	6.0	60.0	6.5	11.0	5.0	4.5	16.5	8.0	7.0	6.5	118.5
16	5.0	12.0	5.5	66.0	5.0	10.5	4.5	4.0	14.5	12.0	4.0	5.0	120.0
17	5.0	11.5	4.0	63.0	7.5	9.5	3.5	5.0	17.0	7.5	8.5	5.5	118.5
18	6.0	10.5	4.5	51.0	8.0	9.5	4.5	5.0	15.5	9.0	6.5	7.5	107.0
19	5.5	11.0	5.0	56.0	6.5	8.0	10.5	4.5	18.0	7.0	7.5	6.0	119.0
20	4.0	8.5	5.5	62.0	5.0	8.5	5.0	5.0	16.0	6.5	7.0	5.0	103.0

EXHIBIT 21.2   Number of Working Days for Activity Completion for CCC

Home	Exc.	Con.	S&W	Str.	Ele.	W&C	RPI	FPI	R&S	IF	BW	OF	House Time
21	5.0	10.5	5.0	46.0	4.0	9.0	2.5	5.5	15.0	13.0	6.0	5.5	100.0
22	4.5	11.5	5.5	57.0	5.0	8.5	4.5	3.5	17.5	7.5	9.0	6.5	102.0
23	5.0	13.0	6.5	68.0	5.5	10.0	6.0	5.0	20.0	9.5	10.0	8.0	123.5
24	5.5	11.0	3.5	65.0	4.5	11.5	3.5	4.5	15.5	5.5	6.5	7.0	119.5
25	4.5	11.5	6.0	55.0	9.5	10.5	7.0	5.0	14.0	8.5	8.0	6.0	101.0
26	5.0	11.5	4.0	63.0	7.5	9.5	3.5	5.0	17.0	7.5	8.5	5.5	118.5
27	6.0	10.5	4.5	51.0	8.0	9.5	4.5	5.0	15.5	9.0	6.5	7.5	107.0
28	5.5	11.0	5.0	56.0	6.5	8.0	10.5	4.5	18.0	7.0	7.5	6.0	119.0
29	4.0	8.5	5.5	62.0	5.0	8.5	5.0	5.0	16.0	6.5	7.0	5.0	103.0
30	5.5	11.5	4.5	64.0	3.5	9.5	13.5	6.5	15.0	7.5	4.5	6.5	111.0
31	5.0	11.0	5.0	54.0	5.0	10.0	6.0	5.0	14.5	10.5	6.0	8.0	112.0
32	4.5	12.5	6.0	60.0	6.5	11.0	5.0	4.5	16.5	8.0	7.0	6.5	118.5
33	5.0	12.0	5.5	66.0	5.0	10.5	4.5	4.0	14.5	12.0	4.0	5.0	120.0
34	5.0	11.0	4.0	58.0	4.5	9.0	5.0	5.0	15.5	5.0	7.5	7.0	107.0
35	6.0	7.0	6.5	67.0	4.0	11.0	3.0	6.0	15.5	7.5	8.0	6.5	120.0
36	4.0	11.5	5.0	60.0	4.0	9.5	5.0	5.5	14.0	8.0	7.0	7.5	110.5
37	4.5	12.0	4.5	53.0	7.0	7.5	8.5	4.5	16.0	6.5	5.5	9.0	100.5
38	4.5	10.0	4.5	60.0	5.0	9.5	7.5	6.0	18.5	8.0	7.0	9.5	116.5
39	6.0	12.5	5.0	58.0	4.5	9.0	9.0	5.5	15.0	7.0	5.0	11.0	104.0
40	5.0	10.0	4.0	57.0	5.5	8.5	6.0	4.5	16.5	6.0	9.5	6.5	106.5

CCC management would like to know the expected completion time for a house if a project manager were to be hired. In addition, there is interest in knowing what the typical schedule for building a house would look like in this situation. This can be dealt with by producing a project schedule that assumes that each activity will take its expected completion time. This project schedule should also show the associated earliest times that each activity can start and finish, and the latest times that each activity can start and finish. These latest activity start and finish times should reflect the target completion of a house in its expected completion time.

The hiring of a project manager could be justified on a cost basis if the expected completion time for a house could be sufficiently reduced from the current scenario, as represented by the average completion time for building a house in the existing situation. There is a fixed cost of $350 per day, for each day of construction on each house. This cost results from premiums for insurance against damage to the house while it is under construction, from leasing costs for equipment that must remain at the building site during construction, and other related costs. The general manager would like to know the expected cost savings that would result from employing a project manager who would use the basic notions of project scheduling to keep the timing of the schedule for the construction of each house under control. In order to get some idea of the capacity to build houses, the manager also would like an estimate of the probability that it would take 112 workdays or more to build a house, with a project manager on the job.

Case Twenty-Two

Breakthrough Entrepreneurial Enterprises

Breakthrough Entrepreneurial Enterprises (BEE) is a well-established firm that completely develops ideas for new consumer products for inventors who lack the capital and the business knowledge to develop their proposed products on their own. The resource base that is typically required for developing a new consumer product is prohibitive for the vast majority of individual inventors to even consider. When an individual has developed a preliminary design for a new consumer product, BEE will initially do some marketing research to evaluate its potential for financial success. If it is determined that there is a good chance of success for the proposed product, BEE will then enter into a formal partnership with the designer.

BEE's function in this partnership will be to complete all aspects of product development and to provide all associated financial support, all the way through bringing the product to the consumer market. There are obviously some limitations on the types of products that BEE can consider for development, and most of their projects have centered on products that are targeted for household use. Given the history of the firm and the wide variety of different product lines that they have developed, BEE management has an extensive knowledge of all aspects of the product development process. The firm has developed its own formal model for bringing a product through the entire new product development process.

There are 15 steps in the product development procedure that is used by BEE:

Initial Design (ID). In this phase, BEE's Research and Development group works with the original designer to develop plans for a preliminary model of the proposed product.

Marketing Analysis (MA). This is a first-stage attempt by the marketing group to perform research regarding the characteristics of the particular product that consumers will find appealing.

Prototype Development (PD). After ID is completed, a working model of the initial design is created in this phase. Any possible design flaws are detected through testing and additional analysis.

Final Design (FD). The final design stage comes after PD and MA, to integrate design issues from PD with product characteristics that consumers consider as being important from MA.

Test Procedures (TP). After PD has been completed, the most critical characteristics of the product design can be identified, and acceptable bounds on these characteristics are then established for use in final product testing.

Preliminary Process Analysis (PP). Once PD has been completed, a preliminary plan can be developed to determine the basics of the processes that will be used to produce the product. This would include an analysis of processes that other BEE facilities already specialize in, and of the possible use of these BEE facilities if they currently have excess capacity that is available for the proposed product.

Cost Estimates (CE). Cost estimates for producing the product can be determined once it has been fully defined during FD and some input on the production process has been gained after PP is complete.

Test Development (TD). In this stage, the details of the actual testing procedures that will be used to test the critical product characteristics are determined. This testing will measure the characteristics that are established after the completion of TP, with some possible modifications that result from the completion of FD.

Market Forecast (MF). After the completion of CE and all of the activities that precede it, the product characteristics are established and a cost estimate for the product is available. The marketing group then obtains estimates of the ultimate demand for the particular product during the MF stage.

Advertising Plan (AP). Once the MF phase is complete, the marketing group develops general plans for advertising the product.

Process Selection (PS). The final determination of process selection for producing the product is made once the product is finally defined and the ultimate capacity requirements are known. This requires that MF and all of its preceding activities have been completed.

Initial Production Run (IP). The production system is set up, and a preliminary run is made to initiate the operating facility. This step can only be performed after both TD and PS are completed.

System Testing (ST). This phase fine-tunes the production system, once the basic production system is operating, after the completion of IP.

Advertising Campaign (AC). The advertising campaign for the product is initiated after it is certain that the existing production system can produce the product to the established specifications, with the completion of ST. This stage also requires that AP has been completed.

Full-Scale Production (FS). Once the production system is known to be operating properly, it goes through a process to gear it up to full-scale production of the product. This step is started after ST has been completed.

All of the stated activity precedence relations on the activities in the product development process must be maintained, along with all precedence relations that they imply. Two activities can be worked on concurrently in the absence of a precedence relation between them.

BEE management is currently considering the development of a new idea that has been brought to them for consideration, and preliminary analysis shows that the idea has a great deal of potential. The problem is that there are some concerns that other firms might be developing a similar product. As a result, BEE management wants to know how long it should be expected to take to get this product through their entire product development cycle.

Some information has been gathered to aid management in answering this question. Exhibit 22.1 shows the time, in weeks, that it took for each step of the product development process for 25 projects that BEE handled that are considered to be characteristic of the nature of the currently proposed product. There are no observations from unusual events in the data from Exhibit 22.1. There are enough observations in Exhibit 22.1 to obtain good estimates of optimistic, most likely, and pessimistic completion

EXHIBIT 22.1   Activity Times, in Weeks, for 25 BEE Product Development Projects

Project	ID	MA	PD	TP	FD	PP	TD	CE	MF	AP	IP	PS	AC	ST	FS
1	3	2	1	5	6	4	3	2	7	10	3	11	6	1	1
2	7	6	3	3	3	2	6	1	9	2	5	9	5	2	6
3	9	7	2	1	5	5	4	2	10	9	2	4	3	8	3
4	8	9	2	11	14	6	8	7	6	11	5	6	4	3	4
5	6	13	2	3	6	4	5	2	8	8	4	8	2	2	4
6	8	3	3	2	9	7	3	1	11	6	7	5	5	1	4
7	7	11	1	4	3	5	4	2	7	6	9	2	7	2	7
8	2	9	2	4	11	8	1	3	4	6	3	7	5	2	4
9	8	12	2	1	5	5	6	8	8	4	6	7	6	6	3
10	9	7	3	3	8	5	9	15	10	6	1	7	5	3	4
11	8	8	1	6	6	4	5	1	9	1	11	10	5	2	6
12	4	4	2	4	4	5	4	3	9	4	5	7	7	1	5
13	8	8	2	10	9	5	5	2	8	6	13	7	5	2	4
14	9	9	3	2	4	5	6	6	8	10	5	7	8	9	4
15	8	8	1	2	13	6	5	2	12	4	4	7	4	1	4
16	7	8	2	3	15	7	7	4	5	6	15	7	5	2	5
17	8	14	2	7	6	3	2	13	8	6	14	4	5	8	4
18	1	9	2	1	12	5	5	2	7	1	2	8	5	6	1
19	9	8	3	3	5	2	7	1	8	6	10	7	2	1	4
20	8	4	1	3	7	5	6	10	8	6	6	9	5	2	2
21	9	9	2	9	6	5	2	3	9	8	1	5	6	4	3
22	8	8	2	2	6	5	8	4	5	8	7	12	4	3	4
23	9	11	2	1	4	6	7	2	7	3	3	6	5	1	2
24	5	8	3	8	3	8	4	3	11	11	5	10	3	2	5
25	7	5	1	2	5	3	3	1	6	2	4	3	8	1	7

times for each activity, and these estimates should serve as a basis for obtaining expected activity times and variance for activity times.

BEE management wants to see a schedule that shows the earliest and latest times that each activity can start and finish in order to have the product development cycle for this product completed in one year (52 weeks). These start and finish times should be based on the assumption that each activity will take its associated expected completion time to get done. The late-start and late-finish times for activities should be based on the target completion time of 52 weeks for the project.

BEE management also is fully aware that the project could run longer than the target of 52 weeks due to the natural variation in activity completion times. This is problematic because of the concerns that competitors might be pursuing a similar product. BEE management believes that this product has great potential, and they will consider the use of additional resources to speed up the project if there are serious concerns that it will run over the 52-week target for project completion. As a result, they want an estimate of the probability that the project will run longer than 52 weeks under normal conditions.

Delta Development Company

Delta Development Company (DDC) has been in the business of constructing tract homes for a number of years. DDC is associated with a small oil company in the southwest, and it manages the construction of homes on tracts of land that the company still owns after the wells have been played out. Since the start of the business, DDC has built more than 1,000 homes. DDC employs their own teams of workers in the 12 specialty fields that are required for constructing houses. These specialty areas are:

- Excavation (Exc): This includes all excavation work for the basement and the digging of all trenches for the installation of water and sewer lines.
- Concrete (Con): This includes the preliminary laying of drainage pipes and the pouring of all concrete for the basement, driveway, and basement walls.
- Sewer and Water (S&W): This includes running sewer and water lines from the road to the main hookups in the basement of the house.
- Structure (Str): This includes installation of the living space floor over the basement; putting up studs for all walls, roof, and ceilings; putting on a rough exterior siding; placing a rough waterproof covering over the rough outside siding and roof; installing insulation; and the insertion of all exterior windows and doors.
- Electric (Ele): This includes running the main electric power line to the house, installing the main circuit box and the installation of all wires for the fixtures.
- Rough Plumbing (RPl): This includes the installation of all copper pipes and plastic tubing inside the walls of the structure for all of the sewer and water fixtures.
- Walls and Cabinets (W&C): This includes the application of drywall and the placement of kitchen cabinets.
- Finish Plumbing (FPl): This includes the placement of all plumbing fixtures and a hot water heating system.
- Roofing and Siding (R&S): This includes the installation of the roofing material, rain gutters, and exterior siding over part of the house.
- Inside Finish (IF): This includes plastering, painting, carpeting, trim work, and other activities to complete the inside of the house.

- Brick Work (BW): This includes the application of bricks to parts of the exterior of the house and some decorative stonework around the house.
- Outside Finish (OF): This includes leveling the surrounding yard, spreading a layer of topsoil, planting a lawn, and other landscaping work.

There are some restrictions on the order in which these activities can be completed. Neither Concrete nor Sewer and Water can start until excavation is complete. Structure can only start after Concrete is done. Sewer and Water must be completed before Rough Plumbing can begin. Structure must be done before any of Roofing and Siding, Electric, and Rough Plumbing. Rough Plumbing and Electric must both be completed before Walls and Cabinets can begin. Roofing and Siding must be done before Brick Work, and Brick Work must be done before Outside Finish. Walls and Cabinets must be done before Finish Plumbing, and Finish Plumbing must be done before Inside Finish can start.

There is some variation in the design of homes that are built by DDC, but the amount of work required from each given specialty group is about the same for each house that they work on. There is, however, some natural variation in the completion times for the activities of each of the specialty teams due to factors such as weather problems, availability of needed materials and equipment, and some absenteeism due to illness and injury. Exhibit 23.1 shows the times that were required by each of the work crews to finish their respective activities over the last 20 homes built by DDC. Nothing unusual happened during these observations, and the times represent what should normally be expected. Times are expressed in units of workdays. There are a sufficient number of activity times reported in Exhibit 23.1 so that the data can be used to obtain reasonable estimates of optimistic, most likely, and pessimistic completion times for each activity. These time estimates should be used as the basis of computing expected completion times for each activity.

PROJECT MANAGEMENT PROBLEMS

The general manager is considering the option of making some changes in DDC's operating procedures. Currently, DDC specialty crews are scheduled for work at different sites when they check into the main office after completing work at their latest assigned site. There are concerns as to whether or not this existing scheduling procedure is maintaining adequate control of the system. Exhibit 23.1 shows the total completion times required for finishing the last 20 houses that were built by DDC. Due to the lack of careful supervision over the assignment of work crews to jobs and a lack of monitoring work crew progress at work sites, these total completion times are likely to be more than should be expected. As a result, the general manager is considering the possibility of hiring a project manager. The project manager would be responsible for developing a schedule for when subcontractors should be working on each house, and then keeping track of the progress of the crews at the work sites.

DDC management would like to see some input regarding the type of analysis that a project manager would typically be generating to control the process of constructing of a house. For example, there is interest in seeing what a typical schedule for building

EXHIBIT 23.1 Number of Working Days for Activity Completion for DDC

Home	Exc.	Con.	S&W	Str.	Ele.	W&C	RPI	FPI	R&S	IF	BW	OF	Total Time
1	5.0	11.0	4.0	58.0	4.5	9.0	5.0	5.0	15.5	5.0	7.5	7.0	107.0
2	6.0	7.0	6.5	67.0	4.0	11.0	3.0	6.0	15.5	7.5	8.0	6.5	120.0
3	4.0	11.5	5.0	60.0	4.0	9.5	5.0	5.5	14.0	8.0	7.0	7.5	110.5
4	4.5	12.0	4.5	53.0	7.0	7.5	8.5	4.5	16.0	6.5	5.5	9.0	100.5
5	5.0	10.5	5.0	46.0	4.0	9.0	2.5	5.5	15.0	13.0	6.0	5.5	100.0
6	4.5	11.5	5.5	57.0	5.0	8.5	4.5	3.5	17.5	7.5	9.0	6.5	102.0
7	5.0	13.0	6.5	68.0	5.5	10.0	6.0	5.0	20.0	9.5	10.0	8.0	123.5
8	5.5	11.0	3.5	65.0	4.5	11.5	3.5	4.5	15.5	5.5	6.5	7.0	119.5
9	4.5	11.5	6.0	55.0	9.5	10.5	7.0	5.0	14.0	8.5	8.0	6.0	101.0
10	4.5	10.0	4.5	60.0	5.0	9.5	7.5	6.0	18.5	8.0	7.0	9.5	116.5
11	6.0	12.5	5.0	58.0	4.5	9.0	9.0	5.5	15.0	7.0	5.0	11.0	104.0
12	5.0	10.0	4.0	57.0	5.5	8.5	6.0	4.5	16.5	6.0	9.5	6.5	106.5
13	5.5	11.5	4.5	64.0	3.5	9.5	13.5	6.5	15.0	7.5	4.5	6.5	111.0
14	5.0	11.0	5.0	54.0	5.0	10.0	6.0	5.0	14.5	10.5	6.0	8.0	112.0
15	4.5	12.5	6.0	60.0	6.5	11.0	5.0	4.5	16.5	8.0	7.0	6.5	118.5
16	5.0	12.0	5.5	66.0	5.0	10.5	4.5	4.0	14.5	12.0	4.0	5.0	120.0
17	5.0	11.5	4.0	63.0	7.5	9.5	3.5	5.0	17.0	7.5	8.5	5.5	118.5
18	6.0	10.5	4.5	51.0	8.0	9.5	4.5	5.0	15.5	9.0	6.5	7.5	107.0
19	5.5	11.0	5.0	56.0	6.5	8.0	10.5	4.5	18.0	7.0	7.5	6.0	119.0
20	4.0	8.5	5.5	62.0	5.0	8.5	5.0	5.0	16.0	6.5	7.0	5.0	103.0

a house would look like in this situation. Developing a schedule that assumes that each activity will take its expected completion time would be adequate to meet this request. This schedule should include the associated earliest times that each activity can start and finish, and the latest times that each activity can start and finish. These latest activity start and finish times should be based upon using the expected completion time for the house as the target completion time.

The hiring of a project manager could be justified on a cost basis if the expected total construction time for completing a house could be sufficiently reduced from the current situation. There is a fixed cost of $250 per day for each day of construction on each house. This cost results from premiums for insurance against damage to the house while it is under construction, from leasing costs for equipment that must remain at the building site during construction, and other related costs. The general manager would like to know the expected cost savings, on a per house basis, that would result from employing a project manager who would use the basic notions of project scheduling to keep the timing of the schedule for the construction of each house under control, relative to the existing situation.

TROUBLE IN SOLAR CITY

DDC is also in the early stages of building a new development of tract homes. The houses in this development, Solar City, will be nearly identical to the basic structure of other DDC homes. The major distinction of the Solar City units is that they will each have a solar-assisted heating system. This system is typical of many solar-assisted systems that are in use. In particular, a series of liquid-filled coils of tubing is placed in solar heat collector boxes on the roof. The tubing then carries the solar heated liquid from the coils on the roof to the basement with the aid of a small pump. In the basement, a heat exchanger transfers heat from the solar heated liquid in the tubes to the water that is used in the primary heating system for the house.

The solar-assisted system cannot heat the house completely on its own, but it can significantly reduce the demands for heat from the boiler that is used to heat the water for the heating system. DDC workers have not installed these solar assisted heating units in any other developments, so there is limited data available about installation times for this activity. To date, DDC has installed 26 solar heating units that are exactly like those to be used in the Solar City project. Exhibit 23.2 shows the amount of time that was required to install each of the solar heating systems.

Since the solar collector boxes are mounted on the roof, it is required that Roofing and Siding must be completed before the solar work begins. To avoid damage to the finished house, solar work must be completed before Inside Finish can begin. Problems also develop if the Solar crew and the Finish Plumbing crew attempt to work on the same house at the same time. Both of these crews require access to the same areas of the house, both are competing for the same resources and tools, and DDC has some employees acting as members of both types of crews. As things currently stand, it is not feasible to have any overlap in the times during which the Solar and Finish Plumbing crews are working on the same house. The general manager would like to have information regarding the best sequence of scheduling for the Solar and Finish Plumbing crews for houses in the Solar City development.

EXHIBIT 23.2
Working Days for Solar Installation

Home	Time
1	12.5
2	12.0
3	11.0
4	10.0
5	9.0
6	8.0
7	8.5
8	7.0
9	5.5
10	4.0
11	6.0
12	4.5
13	5.0
14	5.5
15	6.5
16	5.5
17	4.0
18	6.0
19	5.0
20	5.5
21	5.5
22	6.5
23	5.0
24	7.0
25	4.5
26	6.0

The general manager also realizes that the expected construction time for houses in Solar City could be reduced if some modifications were made to the construction process to allow for the overlap of the Solar and Finish Plumbing activities; that is, if modifications were made to allow these two crews to concurrently work on the same house. Of particular interest is the maximum additional expected cost, on a per house basis, that DDC should be willing to accept to initiate the modifications to the construction process to allow the Solar and Finish Plumbing activities to overlap. If the expected savings that result from the associated reduction in the total completion time for a house is greater than the cost for allowing overlap of these two activities, the DDC manager might pursue the option to allow for overlap.

There will naturally be some variability in the completion times of both the Solar and Finish Plumbing activities, and their associated time of overlap for any given house. However, the maximum allowable cost for permitting these activities to run concurrently can be based on the additional savings that is expected when the Solar and Finish Plumbing activities are allowed to overlap, and each activity uses its expected completion time as its actual time.

Eller Electrical Products

Eller Electrical Products (EEP) is a well-established firm with a number of branches that are located primarily on the East Coast of the United States. The original headquarters of the firm is located in North Carolina, and the primary business focus of the firm is the development and production of electrical products for household use. Typical product lines include hair dryers, food processors, and electric space heaters. Given the long history of the firm and the wide variety of different product lines that they have developed, EEP management has a thorough knowledge of all aspects of the new product development process.

EEP has developed a 15-step model of the product development procedure that they use for all new products:

Initial Design (ID): In this phase, the research and development group works to design plans for a preliminary model of the product in question.

Marketing Analysis (MA): This is a first-stage attempt by the marketing group to perform some research to identify the particular product characteristics that consumers will find appealing.

Prototype Development (PD): After ID has been completed, a working model of the initial design is created. Any possible design flaws are detected in this phase through testing and additional analysis.

Final Design (FD): The final design stage comes after both PD and MA have been completed, to integrate design issues from PD with the product characteristics that consumers consider as being important from MA.

Test Procedures (TP): After PD has been completed, the most critical structural characteristics of the product design can be identified, and acceptable bounds on these characteristics are then established, for use during final product testing.

Preliminary Process Analysis (PP): Once PD has been completed, a preliminary plan can be developed to determine the basics of the processes that will be used to produce the product. This would include an analysis of processes that EEP already specializes in, and of the possible use of other EEP facilities that currently have excess capacity available for the new product.

Cost Estimates (CE): Cost estimates for producing the product can be determined once it has been fully defined during FD and some input on the production process has been gained after PP is complete.

Test Development (TD): In this stage, the details of the actual testing procedures that will be used to test the critical product characteristics are determined. This testing will measure the characteristics that were established during TP, with some possible modifications that result from the completion of FD.

Market Forecast (MF): After the completion of CE and all of the activities that precede it, the product characteristics are well established and all cost estimates for the product are available. The marketing group then obtains estimates of the ultimate demand for this particular product during the MF stage.

Advertising Plan (AP): Once the MF phase is complete, the marketing group then starts to develop general plans for advertising the product.

Process Selection (PS): The final determination of process selection for producing the product is made once the product characteristics are finally defined and the ultimate capacity requirements are known from demand estimates. This requires that MF and all of its preceding activities have been completed.

Initial Production Run (IP): The production system is set up in this stage, and a preliminary "shakedown" run is made to initiate the operating facility. This step can be performed only after both TD and PS have been completed.

System Testing (ST): This phase fine-tunes the production system, once the basic production system is operating, after the completion of IP.

Advertising Campaign (AC): The advertising campaign for the product is launched after it is certain that the existing production system can produce the product to the established specifications, with the completion of ST. This stage also requires that AP has been completed.

Full Scale Production (FS): Once the basic production system is known to be operating properly, it then goes through a process to gear it up to full-scale production of the product. This step is started after ST has been completed.

All of the stated activity precedence relations on the activities in the product development process must be maintained, along with all precedence relations that they imply. Any activities can be worked on concurrently in the absence of any precedence relation between them.

EEP is currently considering the development of a new idea that a worker in their research and development group has discovered. The basic development behind this new product concept would involve extending and adapting some components from currently existing EEP products. The proposed product would quickly start charcoal fires in barbecue grills by using an electrical process that would not require the use of any chemical fluids. The proposed product is initially being called the Phoenix Fire Starter by EEP management.

As far as EEP staff is aware, none of their competitors are working on any product of this type at any level. The plan of EEP management is to start immediately to develop a schedule to design, produce and ship the Phoenix, so as to capture the market. There is a strong desire to manage this product development process, in order to contain the total product development cost, and information has been gathered to assist in this process. The information comes in the form of activity completion time estimates and their associated costs. These estimates come from an analysis of a number of past EEP projects that were quite similar in their general nature to the Phoenix project.

Exhibit 24.1 gives a summary of these estimated results that are related to each of the 15 activities in EEP's new product development model. The "Normal Time" estimates represent the expected number of weeks that each activity would take under typical circumstances, when no unusual measures are taken to speed up the associated activity. The "Crash Time" estimates indicate the number of weeks for the fastest possible time for completion of each activity, while using all reasonable efforts to speed up the activity completion. The project manager can essentially choose the number of weeks to allow for each of these product development activities, with allowable activity times ranging from the Crash Time to the Normal Time for each associated activity.

Of course, some expediting cost is associated with speeding up the completion time for any activity. That expediting cost is different for each activity since different measures must be taken to reduce activity times for each of the different activities. Estimated total costs are given for activity completion in the Normal Time and in the Crash Time for each activity. Since no extreme measures are considered in reducing activity times to their respective Crash Times, it is reasonable to assume that the expediting cost to reduce any of the activity completion times will increase in an approximately linear fashion from the Normal Time completion to the Crash Time completion.

Some of the activity completion costs in Exhibit 24.1 contain fixed-cost components that are not a function of the duration for the activity. There are also some additional fixed costs that have not been included in the activity completion costs, since these do not have any impact on determining the least-cost timing for the product development process. EEP management knows that the time and cost estimates in Exhibit 24.1 are not perfect. However, these estimates can be assumed to be relatively reliable due to the firm's long history of developing similar types of products.

EXHIBIT 24.1 Activity Times (Weeks) and Associated Costs for the Phoenix Project	**Activity**	**Crash Time**	**Normal Time**	**Crash Cost**	**Normal Cost**
	ID	4	11	$425,500	$105,600
	MA	6	9	$325,000	$64,900
	PD	1	3	$115,100	$42,900
	PP	4	7	$95,000	$42,200
	FD	3	7	$400,000	$95,200
	TP	2	5	$83,000	$30,200
	TD	2	9	$284,000	$41,100
	CE	2	5	$67,000	$27,400
	MF	5	10	$287,000	$38,000
	AP	3	9	$232,000	$32,800
	IP	4	8	$392,000	$82,800
	PS	3	9	$223,000	$44,200
	AC	3	9	$445,000	$53,200
	ST	1	4	$275,000	$75,800
	FS	2	5	$301,000	$118,300

The EEP manager who is in charge of this product initially wants to know the crash time for the entire project, which is the fastest possible time in which the Phoenix project could be completed. As mentioned before, containing the cost of this product development project is a primary concern. Thus, another piece of information that is of significant interest to the project manager is the number of weeks of project completion time that will minimize the total project cost, along with the associated number of weeks to allocate for each activity.

This question cannot be answered by simply finding the project completion time that would result when each activity is performed in its Normal Time in order to minimize the sum of activity completion costs. This results from the fact that it is estimated that EEP is forgoing $65,000 per week in profit for every week until the project is complete. This profit is forgone because projected revenues from sales of the product will not be received until the Phoenix project is completed through both the Advertising Campaign and Full Scale Production. This forgone profit is not accounted for in any of the activity completion cost estimates in Exhibit 24.1.

The Phoenix project is considered to be quite promising by EEP management, and there is a possibility that the project might be accelerated from the least-total-cost completion time. As a result, there is an interest in knowing how much total project costs would increase as a result of speeding up completion time for the project from the least-cost completion time. To examine the cost sensitivity of such a decision, the manager wants to know the total minimum project completion cost that would be incurred for all four-week project duration increments, starting with the least-total-cost number of weeks, down to the previously established crash completion time for the project. The number of weeks that should be allocated to each activity should also be given to achieve the minimum total cost for each of these project duration targets.

Fox Hill Development

Fox Hill Development (FHD) has been in the business of constructing single-family residential homes for a number of years. FHD selectively acquires large parcels of property in different geographic areas and then oversees the construction of all homes in the resulting development after the parcel is approved for subdivision by local government authorities. Since the start of the business, FHD has built more than 2,000 homes. FHD employs their own specialized teams of workers to do work in the 12 specialty fields that are required for constructing houses. FHD finds that it is beneficial to have these specialty teams as their own employees, rather than being reliant on independent subcontractors. This is particularly important when there is a critical need to get one of these activities completed on a priority basis.

The 12 specialty areas are:

- Excavation (Exc): This includes all necessary excavation for the basement and digging all trenches for the placement of water and sewer lines.
- Concrete (Con): This activity includes the preliminary laying of drainpipe below the basement floor, and the pouring of all concrete for the basement floor, driveway, and basement walls.
- Sewer and Water (S&W): This includes running both the sewer and water lines from the road to the main hookups in the basement.
- Structure (Str): This includes installation of the living space floor over the basement; putting up studs for all walls, roof and ceilings; putting on a rough exterior siding; placing a rough waterproof covering over the rough outside siding and roof; installing insulation; and the insertion of all exterior windows and doors.
- Electric (Ele): This includes running the main electric power line to the house, installing the main circuit box, and running all electrical wires for the fixtures.
- Rough Plumbing (RPl): This includes the installation of all copper pipes and plastic tubing inside the walls of the structure for all sewer and water fixtures.
- Walls and Cabinets (W&C): This includes the application of all drywall and the placement of kitchen cabinets.
- Finish Plumbing (FPl): This includes the placement of all plumbing fixtures and the installation of a hot-water heating system that is the primary heat source for the house.

- Roofing and Siding (R&S): This includes the installation of the roofing material, rain gutters and exterior siding over part of the house.
- Inside Finish (IF): This includes all finish plastering, painting, carpet installation, trim work, and other activities to complete the inside of the house.
- Brick Work (BW): This includes the application of bricks to parts of the exterior of the house and some decorative stonework around the house.
- Outside Finish (OF): This includes the final leveling of the yard area, the spreading of an adequate layer of topsoil, placement of sod for the lawn, and other landscaping work.

There are a number of precedence restrictions on the order in which some of these activities can be completed. Neither Concrete nor Sewer and Water can start until excavation is complete. Structure can only start after Concrete is done. Sewer and Water must be completed before Rough Plumbing can begin. Structure must be completed before any of Roofing and Siding, Electric, and Rough Plumbing can begin. Rough Plumbing and Electric must both be completed before Walls and Cabinets can be started. Roofing and Siding must be done before Brick Work, and Brick Work must be done before Outside Finish can begin. Walls and Cabinets must be done before Finish Plumbing, and both Finish Plumbing and Roofing and Siding must be done before Inside Finish can start.

The homes built by FHD do have some limited variation in their design, but the amount of work required from any given specialty group is effectively the same for each house that FHD builds. There has been variation in the completion times for activities of the specialty teams for different houses. The overriding factor for activity completion time has been the amount of time that FHD has allowed the specialty teams to complete the specific activities in each particular case. Specialty teams report in at the completion of work on each house, and they are assigned to work at another site. At that time they are told how many workdays they have available to get the activity completed. By resorting to the use of overtime, second-shift work, rental of extra equipment, and other methods, each of the specialty team supervisors has generally been able to meet the activity time limitations that have been imposed on them by FHD for each specific house. Exhibit 25.1 shows the activity times that were assigned to each of the specialty teams over the last 20 homes built by FHD. The differences in the activity times for different houses are not due to conditions such as weather, but simply reflect the amount of time that specialty teams were assigned for completion of their respective activities in each specific house. Nothing unusual happened during these observations, and the assigned activity times represent the range of what could normally be expected. Times are expressed in units of workdays.

Exhibit 25.2 shows the associated specialty team costs to FHD to have the activities completed within the times that were specified by FHD for each of the last 20 houses. The costs in Exhibit 25.2 include fixed costs for materials that are used in the associated activities. For example, the costs associated with structural work include all cost for lumber, trusses, and other structural material. As might be expected, the cost to have an activity completed in a shorter amount of time is generally greater than what would be expected if more time were to be allowed for completion. Obviously, there is an upper limit on how much can be saved by allowing more time to do an activity, and

EXHIBIT 25.1 Number of Working Days Allocated for Specialty Group Activities

Home	Exc.	Con.	S&W	Str.	Ele.	W&C	RPI	FPI	R&S	IF	BW	OF
1	5.0	11.0	4.0	58.0	4.5	9.0	5.0	5.0	15.5	5.0	7.5	7.0
2	6.0	7.0	6.5	67.0	4.0	11.0	3.0	6.0	15.5	7.5	8.0	6.5
3	4.0	11.5	5.0	60.0	4.0	9.5	5.0	5.5	14.0	8.0	7.0	7.5
4	4.5	12.0	4.5	53.0	7.0	7.5	8.5	4.5	16.0	6.5	5.5	9.0
5	5.0	10.5	5.0	46.0	4.0	9.0	2.5	5.5	15.0	13.0	6.0	5.5
6	4.5	11.5	5.5	57.0	5.0	8.5	4.5	3.5	17.5	7.5	9.0	6.5
7	5.0	13.0	6.5	68.0	5.5	10.0	6.0	5.0	20.0	9.5	10.0	8.0
8	5.5	11.0	3.5	65.0	4.5	11.5	3.5	4.5	15.5	5.5	6.5	7.0
9	4.5	11.5	6.0	55.0	9.5	10.5	7.0	5.0	14.0	8.5	8.0	6.0
10	4.5	10.0	4.5	60.0	5.0	9.5	7.5	6.0	18.5	8.0	7.0	9.5
11	6.0	12.5	5.0	58.0	4.5	9.0	9.0	5.5	15.0	7.0	5.0	11.0
12	5.0	10.0	4.0	57.0	5.5	8.5	6.0	4.5	16.5	6.0	9.5	6.5
13	5.5	11.5	4.5	64.0	3.5	9.5	13.5	6.5	15.0	7.5	4.5	6.5
14	5.0	11.0	5.0	54.0	5.0	10.0	6.0	5.0	14.5	10.5	6.0	8.0
15	4.5	12.5	6.0	60.0	6.5	11.0	5.0	4.5	16.5	8.0	7.0	6.5
16	5.0	12.0	5.5	66.0	5.0	10.5	4.5	4.0	14.5	12.0	4.0	5.0
17	5.0	11.5	4.0	63.0	7.5	9.5	3.5	5.0	17.0	7.5	8.5	5.5
18	6.0	10.5	4.5	51.0	8.0	9.5	4.5	5.0	15.5	9.0	6.5	7.5
19	5.5	11.0	5.0	56.0	6.5	8.0	10.5	4.5	18.0	7.0	7.5	6.0
20	4.0	8.5	5.5	62.0	5.0	8.5	5.0	5.0	16.0	6.5	7.0	5.0

EXHIBIT 25.2 Costs for Associated Specialty Group Activities (in Dollars)

Home	Exc.	Con.	S&W	Str.	Ele.	W&C	RPI	FPI	R&S	IF	BW	OF
1	5,438	4,531	5,210	19,213	5,757	8,317	7,740	5,989	6,988	5,859	5,507	6,408
2	4,822	6,451	3,708	18,013	5,679	7,297	7,987	5,804	6,839	5,401	5,786	6,499
3	6,105	4,434	4,693	18,775	5,611	8,002	7,476	6,187	7,049	5,188	5,975	6,317
4	5,635	4,170	4,887	20,503	4,439	8,478	6,548	6,637	6,745	5,821	6,689	6,180
5	5,520	4,756	5,017	20,716	5,541	7,018	8,346	5,724	7,302	4,177	6,289	6,511
6	5,670	4,233	4,287	21,254	5,210	7,982	7,879	7,306	6,690	5,070	4,889	6,410
7	5,168	3,857	3,856	18,432	5,368	7,571	7,201	5,956	6,088	4,751	4,836	6,375
8	5,079	4,955	5,683	18,789	5,766	7,088	7,752	6,461	6,917	5,488	5,904	6,436
9	5,988	4,386	4,154	19,612	3,931	7,634	6,888	5,939	7,126	4,855	5,751	6,400
10	5,838	5,235	5,406	19,684	5,377	7,988	6,648	5,868	6,279	5,175	5,847	6,330
11	4,520	4,243	4,502	19,666	5,466	7,912	6,231	5,941	6,849	5,465	6,609	6,077
12	5,283	5,488	4,867	21,255	5,299	8,514	7,148	6,324	6,587	5,399	5,148	6,366
13	5,024	4,741	4,667	18,545	5,766	7,878	4,886	5,258	6,909	5,385	7,221	6,597
14	5,545	4,138	4,945	19,678	5,367	7,977	7,090	5,999	7,228	4,651	6,212	6,568
15	5,609	3,703	4,294	19,676	5,179	7,665	7,731	6,759	6,988	5,188	5,685	6,488
16	5,491	4,432	4,387	17,688	5,553	7,599	7,879	6,679	7,075	4,465	7,435	6,557
17	5,340	4,498	5,457	18,256	4,419	7,980	7,945	6,192	6,544	5,288	5,545	6,533
18	4,391	4,611	4,657	21,135	4,549	8,031	7,588	6,458	6,819	4,998	6,098	6,302
19	5,173	5,587	4,738	19,812	4,941	8,611	5,950	6,438	6,335	5,233	5,065	6,589
20	6,069	5,890	4,675	19,145	5,272	8,354	7,458	6,356	6,988	5,222	5,830	6,554

no additional savings can be expected if more time is allowed than the maximum activity times that have been observed.

It can be seen that different activity costs can be incurred for different situations with the same activity completion time. These variations result from conditions, such as weather, that existed at the time the respective activities were completed. The specialty teams completed their activities in the assigned times in each case, and conditions such as weather required different measures, and associated costs, in order to meet the assigned completion time for the activity. No extreme measures were taken to meet the assigned times during these observations, and FHD does not wish to consider doing so at any time in the future.

PROJECT MANAGEMENT PROBLEMS

FHD management is considering the option of making some changes in its operating procedures. Currently, specialty crews are scheduled for work at different sites when they check into the main office after completing work at their previous assigned site. The project management procedure function is not well organized, and the general manager is considering the possibility of improving the procedure of scheduling work crews in order to gain control of the process and to help reduce costs. The problem is complicated by the fact that there is a fixed cost of $450 per day, for each workday of construction on each house, until the house is completed. This cost results from insurance premiums against damage to the house while under construction, from equipment leasing costs for equipment that must remain at the building site during construction, and other related costs. This fixed cost is not included in the activity costs that are given in Exhibit 25.2.

The general manager would like to know the total number of days, and the associated activity time to be scheduled to each of the specialty work crews, that should be allocated to building each house to minimize total cost. This total cost should include the sum of costs for all of the specialty work groups and the $450 per day cost for each day of the duration of the project.

If demand becomes particularly high during some period, the specialty work crews could work on a crash time basis to get the houses done as quickly as possible. Obviously, there are limits on how fast each crew can complete their respective activities. The minimum observed completion time for each activity in Exhibit 25.1 can be assumed to represent the crash time for the associated activity. The manager wants to know the crash completion time for a house, that is, the minimum time it would take to complete a house, which does not necessarily require every activity to be completed in its shortest possible time. In addition, the manager would like to know the minimum additional cost that would be incurred by reducing the number of days allowed for completion of a house, in five-workday increments, from the least-total-cost-construction time down to the crash time to build a house. It is of interest to know the number of workdays that will be assigned for each specialty work crew for each target total completion time as the number of workdays is reduced by five-workday increments.

Facility Location

Kepner Regional Health Center

Kepner County covers a very large area that is approximately 100 miles by 100 miles, and it is located in a sparsely populated region of a western state. The current availability of health care in the county is extremely limited. This is due largely to the fact that the entire county only has about 6,000 residents. This population is spread over 10 primary communities in the county: Aurand (L1), Harman (L2), Clelland (L3), Cornell (L4), Maxham (L5), Gunn (L6), Eason (L7), Jenks (L8), Brownell (L9), and Linda (L10). The current population statistics of each of these communities have been compiled and they are shown in Exhibit 26.1.

All residents certainly do not live at the population centers of their respective communities, but most residents are generally concentrated near the centers. A map of the county was laid out with grid coordinates to measure the relative location of each of these communities. Exhibit 26.1 shows the grid coordinates, scaled in miles from the origin of the grid, for each community center. The X-Coordinate measures the relative East-West distance within the county and the Y-Coordinate measures the relative North-South distance within the county. It is clear from Exhibit 26.1 that the communities in Kepner County have a substantial variation in population, given the fact that they are all small towns, and that they are spread throughout the county.

EXHIBIT 26.1
Population and Grid Coordinates for Kepner County Communities

Location	Population	X	Y
L1	1,000	15	90
L2	300	35	85
L3	700	30	75
L4	400	20	50
L5	200	40	10
L6	1,300	25	60
L7	600	75	80
L8	400	80	40
L9	600	90	5
L10	500	95	85

A PROPOSAL FOR A HEALTH CARE CENTER

The commissioners of Kepner County have recently received some very good news. Federal and state grants have been made available for remote counties to establish health care centers. These centers will not serve to replace hospitals, but they will be capable of dealing with routine health care treatments and counseling, giving physical exams and tests, and dealing with initial care for most noncritical emergency cases like broken bones and bad cuts. Critical injuries will still be dealt with by having patients being sent by helicopter transport to a distant hospital.

The opening of such a health care facility is deeply desired by county residents, since any person with a noncritical injury that requires medical care currently has to face a very long car or ambulance ride to a distant hospital for treatment. The county commissioners have tentatively named the proposed health care facility Kepner Regional Health Center (KRH).

The county commissioners are currently dealing with ways of obtaining funding to support the county's share of financing for KRH. Another very critical issue that faces the commissioners is the determination as to where the facility should be located. There are three commissioners, and all three have very different opinions as to the criteria that should be used to determine the ultimate location for KRH. This is obviously a very politically sensitive decision within the county, so the commissioners have been asked to provide some rationale to justify their positions.

THREE OPINIONS ON LOCATION CRITERIA

Commissioner 1: The facility has to be built in the location that is "most efficient," in the sense that it will minimize the total number of miles that must be traveled by all of patients who require services from KRH.

The location of the position that is suggested by Commissioner 1 would be extremely difficult to identify with complete accuracy. However, many county roads and secondary roads exist throughout Kepner County. As a result, it would be reasonable to assume that the actual driving distance between any of the 10 communities and any proposed location for KRH is proportional to the straight-line distance between the two locations on a map. It would also be quite reasonable to assume that the number of residents from each community that require services from KRH will be directly proportional to the population of the community.

Commissioner 2: Efficiency measures like those proposed by Commissioner 1 are fine when you are talking about shipping widgets from Point A to Point B. However, when a parent has a child with a broken leg, they feel a lot of distress if they have to drive 20 miles for emergency assistance. If they have to drive 40 miles instead, the level of distress would not double, it would increase by a whole lot more than that. With the proposal of Commissioner 1, residents of smaller outlying communities could routinely be put through such extreme distress in emergency situations. The "true distance" between communities and KRH should not be measured as the straight-line distance on a map for such emergencies, but as the squared value of that distance. The fact that patients from the larger population centers might have to drive a few extra miles for a routine physical as a result of this is not nearly as critical by comparison.

Commissioner 3: Commissioners 1 and 2 both raise very valid arguments. However, my staff has done some research to find that most books on the topic of operations management discuss such facility location problems. The consensus is that something called the Centroid Method, or Center of Gravity Method, should typically be used in such service related applications when the objective is to locate a single facility. That approach should certainly be considered in this situation.

The three county commissioners have debated this issue at great length, and they have reached a point that some additional outside input is being sought. As a result, they would like to know the grid coordinates of KRH with each criterion in order to have an idea of just how different the outcome would actually be in each case.

Maledire-Ruth Inc.

Maledire-Ruth, Inc. (MRI), is a well-established firm that can trace its history back to 1918. MRI produces and distributes a product in large volume. MRI has four production facilities that are located near Seattle, Boston, Atlanta, and Denver. Each of these production facilities has a capacity of 500,000 units per year, on a regular-time basis. Unit operating costs are different at each facility due to regional differences in wages that must be paid to workers and to differences in costs that must be paid for raw materials and resources. MRI records have been examined to obtain information about each of these different costs, and all of the results are summarized in Exhibit 27.1.

Each production facility can operate on an overtime basis to produce additional output up to 50% of the regular-time capacity. Since laborers must be paid "time and a half" for overtime, there is a 50% additional premium that must be associated with all labor costs for units that are produced on an overtime basis. In the Seattle production facility, for example, the unit labor cost would increase to $2.355 per unit for all units that are produced on overtime. Material costs are not affected in any way by a switch to overtime production.

The four production facilities each supply product to a distribution site that is located near their own respective production facilities, along with seven other separate MRI distribution sites that are located near Minneapolis, Charleston, New Orleans, Orlando, Philadelphia, Los Angeles, and Kansas City. Unit shipping costs from the production facilities to the 11 different distributor sites depend partly on the relative geographic distance between the production facilities and the distribution sites. However, the availability of bulk shipment by railroad and other modes of transportation have a significant impact on some of these unit-shipping costs. The annual demands at the eleven distribution sites and the associated unit shipping costs from the four production centers are given in Exhibit 27.2.

EXHIBIT 27.1
Summary of MRI Cost Data

Facility Location	Labor Cost per Unit	Material Cost per Unit
Seattle	$1.57	$1.18
Boston	$1.75	$1.20
Atlanta	$1.55	$1.14
Denver	$1.49	$1.16

EXHIBIT 27.2
Demand Requirements at Distribution Sites and Associated Unit Shipping Costs

Distribution Sites	Annual Demand	Seattle	Boston	Atlanta	Denver
Seattle	250,000	0.10	0.45	0.50	0.27
Boston	360,000	0.45	0.10	0.31	0.32
Atlanta	170,000	0.50	0.31	0.10	0.29
Denver	180,000	0.27	0.32	0.29	0.10
Minneapolis	230,000	0.29	0.25	0.27	0.20
Charleston	190,000	0.41	0.24	0.17	0.26
New Orleans	190,000	0.43	0.39	0.20	0.27
Orlando	230,000	0.62	0.35	0.28	0.36
Philadelphia	240,000	0.42	0.21	0.29	0.31
Los Angeles	270,000	0.21	0.43	0.41	0.21
Kansas City	220,000	0.28	0.27	0.26	0.22

MRI has some serious problems to contend with. The first major issue is that the total annual demand for the 11 distribution sites is 2,530,000 units, while the total annual regular-time production capacity at the four production facilities is limited to 2,000,000 units per year. MRI anticipates that the current demand levels will continue, with some minor increases being possible in the future. As a result, MRI is locked into requiring overtime production to meet the anticipated demand.

There are some serious concerns about product quality issues and labor-related issues that are associated with having too heavy a reliance on overtime production on an ongoing basis. Due to the nature of the process that is used by the MRI production facilities, and the associated heavy demands for maintenance on equipment, it is not feasible to operate any facility on a full-time second-shift basis. As a result, there cannot be any additional output from any facility beyond the normal 50% limits of overtime.

The only feasible option that remains open for MRI is the consideration of some capacity expansion. For a number of very good strategic reasons, the firm has limited the consideration of possible locations for capacity expansion to the four locations where it already has production facilities in operation. MRI wishes to determine the internal rate of return on the initial investment that would be obtained from the resulting expected annual-cost savings, after depreciation and taxation, from regular-time capacity expansion of 500,000 units per year at one of the four existing production facilities. The overtime capacity at the expanded facility would also increase by 250,000 units per year, accordingly. The initial cost of this capacity expansion is estimated to be $1,000,000, regardless of the selected location, and the expansion facility will be depreciated over eight years at annual rates of 14%, 25%, 17%, 13%, 9%, 9%, 9%, 4% in successive years. Combined state and federal taxes are paid at a rate of 40%. The realistic lifetime of the project is eight years.

The evaluation of possible expansion locations is made somewhat more complicated since negotiations have led to some significant modifications if the Boston location is selected for expansion. State and local agencies in Massachusetts have made a very strong sales pitch to MRI management. These agencies would incur some one-time expenses on their own, to effectively reduce MRI's initial cost of expansion. Analysis by financial experts indicates that these one-time benefits are equivalent to an immediate after-tax payoff of $250,000. In addition, they would also modify their state and local tax rates. As a result, MRI would only incur a combined state and federal tax rate of 35% on all additional earnings that would result from the total reduction in operating costs if they select the option of expansion in Boston.

There would be no other changes in taxes on the existing facility, just on the additional earnings that would result from the total reduction in operating costs as a result of the expansion. This agreement requires that the facility expansion must have an initial planned investment for expansion of at least $1,000,000. MRI's planned capacity expansion would meet the criteria of the agreement if a 500,000-unit regular-time capacity expansion were to be built there. However, MRI would be able to depreciate only $750,000 in this case. Overall, MRI management finds the Boston offer to sound very appealing from a financial perspective.

The manager of MRI wants to know the best location for expansion, based on the internal rate of return on the initial investment over the eight-year horizon. The internal rate of return should be based on the cost savings that result from the expansion to offset the initial investment, after accounting for depreciation and taxation. The initial investment would be made immediately, with all other expenses and cash inflows being credited at the end of each respective year. The cash savings should be based on the difference in total costs, with and without the capacity expansion. The system should be operated in the most efficient manner possible in both cases for a proper comparison.

It is also possible to split the regular-time capacity expansion equally between two locations. The associated overtime capacities would then increase by 50% of the regular-time capacity expansion. However, this would increase the cost of the initial investment by 25% since construction would have to take place in two different locations. The manager wishes to know the internal rate of return for the best split of capacity expansion in order to know if any increased benefits from doing a split expansion would offset the penalty cost that is incurred for doing so. None of the negotiations regarding the Boston expansion apply if a split facility expansion is done there.

Long Life Battery Company

Long Life Battery Company (LLB) produces dry-cell batteries at five production facilities that are located in New York, Detroit, Seattle, Los Angeles, and Atlanta. All customers acquire product from LLB through distribution centers that are located near each of these facilities, along with three other distribution centers in Phoenix, Kansas City, and Pittsburgh. These three distribution centers do not produce anything for LLB.

As the manager of LLB you have been concerned with the overall operating costs for your firm, and you hired the consulting firm of *S.U.B. Optimizer Systems* to analyze your production-distribution schedule. The executive summary of their report is attached. You have no concern over any of the statements in the summary that are attributed to LLB personnel regarding technical and cost information.

You are currently considering the recommendations of the *S.U.B. Optimizer Systems* report, and want to reach a final decision as to what should be done.

Long Life E

Prepared by S.U.B. Optimizer Systems

LLB has two principle problems to contend with in terms of developing an effective production-distribution schedule to help minimize total operating costs. First, excessive shipping costs have been incurred due to a poor use of shipping patterns. Second, some production facilities are consistently relying on too great a use of overtime to meet demand for the product. Our recommendations for a solution to these problems take place on two levels, and we begin with a solution to deal with shipping costs.

SHIPPING PROBLEMS

The cost of shipping from the five locations in which LLB has production facilities to its eight distribution centers is summarized in Exhibit 28.1. For example, it will cost $0.19 per unit for shipping from the production center in Seattle to the distributor in Los

Angeles. These costs might not appear to be completely consistent with the overall geographic distance between cities. This is due to variability in the availability rail transportation, shipping by water transportation, and other sources of low cost mass shipment at the different sites.

Exhibit 28.2 shows the annual regular time capacities of each of the production centers, along with the annual demand requirements at each of the distribution centers for the next year. Production facilities can operate on an overtime basis for up to 50% of regular-time capacity. For example, Seattle can produce up to 300,000 units/year on regular time and up to 150,000 units/year on overtime.

A linear-programming-based analysis was performed to find shipping patterns to minimize the total annual shipping cost, given the limitations on total capacities for each production facility and the annual requirements of the distribution centers. The

EXHIBIT 28.1 Unit Shipping Costs for Long Life Batteries

				Distribution Centers				
	Sea	LA	Det	NY	Atl	Ph	KC	Pit
Production Centers								
Seattle	.02	.19	.32	.42	.42	.22	.24	.37
Los Angeles	.19	.02	.30	.38	.37	.13	.22	.31
Detroit	.32	.30	.02	.16	.18	.23	.18	.11
New York	.42	.38	.16	.02	.11	.33	.19	.10
Atlanta	.42	.37	.18	.11	.02	.30	.17	.12

EXHIBIT 28.2 Plant Capacities and Distributor Requirements

Location	Regular Time Capacity	Requirements for next year	Projected Annual Growth Rate
Seattle	300,000	130,000	2%
Los Angeles	420,000	400,000	3%
Detroit	370,000	334,000	1%
New York	340,000	445,000	1%
Atlanta	340,000	265,000	2%
Phoenix	—	213,000	2%
Kansas City	—	140,000	2%
Pittsburgh	—	186,000	1%

linear programming formulation is attached in Exhibit 28.3, along with the least-cost solution that was obtained for the problem.

The results of that analysis verify intuition to suggest that we should partition the facilities into three clusters, according to geographic locations. Cluster 1 (Western Region) would contain the production facilities in Los Angeles and Seattle, along with the distribution center in Phoenix. Cluster 2 (Northeast Region) would contain the production centers in Detroit and New York, along with the distribution center in Pittsburgh. Cluster 3 (Southeast Region) would

---

EXHIBIT 28.3 Long Life Battery: Linear Programming Formulation to Minimize Total Annual Shipping Cost

Minimize (Total Annual Shipping Cost)
.02SESE + .19SELA + .32SEDE + .42SENY + .42SEAT + .22SEPH + .24SEKC + .37SEPI + .19LASE + .02LALA + .30LADE + .38LANY + .37LAAT + .13LAPH + .22LAKC + .31LAPI + .32DESE + .30DELA + .02DEDE + .16DENY + .18DEAT + .23DEPH + .18DEKC + .11DEPI + .42NYSE + .38NYLA + .16NYDE + .02NYNY + .11NYAT + .33NYPH + .19NYKC + .10NYPI + .42ATSE + .37ATLA + .18ATDE + .11ATNY + .02ATAT + .30ATPH + .17ATKC + .12ATPI

Subject To

: Limitations on total capacities at production facilities
SESE + SELA + SEDE + SENY + SEAT + SEPH + SEKC + SEPI <= 450,000
LASE + LALA + LADE + LANY + LAAT + LAPH + LAKC + LAPI <= 630,000
DESE + DELA + DEDE + DENY + DEAT + DEPH + DEKC + DEPI <= 555,000
NYSE + NYLA + NYDE + NYNY + NYAT + NYPH + NYKC + NYPI <= 510,000
ATSE + ATLA + ATDE + ATNY + ATAT + ATPH + ATKC + ATPI <= 510,000

: Limitations on demand requirements at distribution centers
SESE + LASE + DESE + NYSE + ATSE >= 130,000
SELA + LALA + DELA + NYLA + ATLA >= 400,000
SEDE + LADE + DEDE + NYDE + ATDE >=334,000
SENY + LANY + DENY + NYNY + ATNY >= 445,000
SEAT + LAAT + DEAT + NYAT + ATAT >= 265,000
SEPH + LAPH + DEPH + NYPH + ATPH >= 213,000
SEKC + LAKC + DEKC + NYKC + ATKC >= 140,000
SEPI + LAPI + DEPI + NYPI + ATPI >= 186,000

Solution

Objective Function Value = $102,780

Variable	Value
SESE	130,000
LALA	400,000
LAPH	213,000
DEDE	334,000
DEPI	121,000
NYNY	445,000
NYPI	65,000
ATAT	265,000
ATKC	140,000

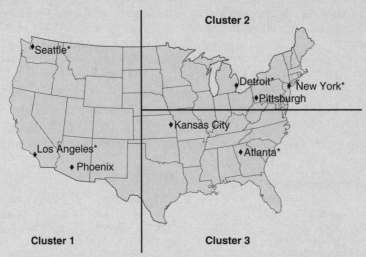

Long Life Battery production-distribution clusters. *Denotes production facility.

contain the production center in Atlanta and the distribution center in Kansas City. All production and shipping would then take place within the respective clusters to minimize total shipping cost. This can be verified by examining the solution that is shown in Exhibit 28.3, where no shipping takes place across any clusters. We recommend implementation of this "cluster system" to help contain shipping costs.

In the next step, we concentrate on the problem of minimizing overtime costs. Exhibit 28.4 shows the unit operating costs for each of the five production facilities, in terms of regular-time labor cost and nonlabor unit variable cost. The nonlabor unit variable cost includes the cost of material and some other production-related expenses. Given standard contract requirements, employees will be paid a 50% pre-

mium for labor on all units that are produced on overtime. For example, the unit cost of regular-time labor is $.22 in Seattle, and this cost will increase to $.33 for each unit that is produced there on overtime. The nonlabor variable operating costs will not change on overtime production. As mentioned above, overtime capacity will be limited to 50% of regular-time capacity.

Exhibit 28.5 shows a spreadsheet that computes the total annual operating cost for LLB with the clustering system in place. This total annual cost consists of the accumulation of labor cost, nonlabor variable cost, and shipping cost. For example, the unit cost for regular-time production in Los Angeles and shipping to Seattle is given as $1.30 in Cluster 1. This unit cost is obtained as the sum of the regular-time production cost in Los Angeles ($.24), the nonlabor variable cost in Los Angeles ($.87), and the shipping cost from Los Angeles to Seattle ($.19). This spreadsheet was used to find that the total operating cost over the three clusters is minimized at $2,409,400, given next year's demand requirements with the clustering system in place.

CAPACITY EXPANSION CONSIDERATIONS

It was mentioned before that some production facilities rely too heavily on the consistent use of overtime production to meet demand. The regular-time capacity limits that are specified in Exhibit 28.2 make

EXHIBIT 28.4 Unit Production Costs at Production Facilities

Location	Regular-Time Labor Cost	Nonlabor Variable Operating Costs
Seattle	.22	.84
Los Angeles	.24	.87
Detroit	.22	.82
New York	.26	.84
Atlanta	.22	.78

EXHIBIT 28.5   Long Life Battery: Least-Total-Cost Solution with the Clustering System in Place

Cluster 1

	Unit Cost					Units Shipped				Remaining
	LA	SE	PH	Capacity		LA	SE	PH	Cost	Capacity
LA-Reg	$1.13	$1.30	$1.24	420,000	LA-Reg	400,000		20,000	$476,800	0
LA-OT	$1.25	$1.42	$1.36	210,000	LA-OT			23,000	$31,280	187,000
SE-Reg	$1.25	$1.08	$1.28	300,000	SE-Reg		130,000	170,000	$358,000	0
SE-OT	$1.36	$1.19	$1.39	150,000	SE-OT				$0	150,000
					Required	400,000	130,000	213,000		
					Shortage	0	0	0		

Total Cost for Cluster 1 = $866,080

Cluster 2

	Unit Cost					Units Shipped				Remaining
	NY	DE	PI	Capacity		NY	DE	PI	Cost	Capacity
NY-Reg	$1.12	$1.26	$1.20	340,000	NY-Reg	340,000			$380,800	0
NY-OT	$1.25	$1.39	$1.33	170,000	NY-OT	105,000			$131,250	65,000
DE-Reg	$1.20	$1.06	$1.18	370,000	DE-Reg		334,000	36,000	$396,520	0
DE-OT	$1.31	$1.17	$1.29	185,000	DE-OT			150,000	$193,500	35,000
					Required	445,000	334,000	186,000		
					Shortage	0	0	0		

Total Cost for Cluster 2 = $1,102,070

Cluster 3

	Unit Cost				Units Shipped			Remaining
	AT	KC	Capacity		AT	KC	Cost	Capacity
AT-Reg	$1.02	$1.17	340,000	AT-Reg	265,000	75,000	$358,050	0
AT-OT	$1.13	$1.28	170,000	AT-OT		65,000	$83,200	105,000
				Required	265,000	140,000		
				Shortage	0	0		

Total Cost for Cluster 3 = $441,250   **Grand Total Cost = $2,409,400**

it quite evident that the facilities in both New York and Los Angeles are particularly having problems. New York must devote 100% of its regular-time output just to meet about 75% of its own projected annual requirement for next year. Similarly, Los Angeles must devote 95% of its regular-time output just to meet its own projected annual requirements for next year. None of the other production facilities have their capacities pushed to such extreme limits, so the consideration of capacity expansion will be limited to the options of expanding capacity in either New York or Los Angeles.

LLB personnel have advised us that capacity expansion is possible at each of the five production facilities, but the analysis from above leads us to conclude that only New York and Los Angeles are serious contenders for consideration. The projected cost of a 150,000-unit annual increase in regular-time output is given as $100,000, with a useful project life of eight years' duration. The associated overtime capacity at any expanded facility would also increase by 75,000 units per year. We understand from your personnel that this 150,000-unit capacity increase cannot be split between different production facilities.

Exhibit 28.6 shows a spreadsheet that gives the production-distribution schedule that minimizes total annual cost over the three clusters if the New York facility has its capacity increased by 150,000 units per year on regular time, and a corresponding overtime capacity increase of 75,000 units per year. The total cost for operating with the increase in capacity at New York is $2,391,700 per year, for a cost

---

EXHIBIT 28.6 Long Life Battery: Least-Total-Cost Solution with the Clustering System in Place and NY Expansion

Cluster 1

	Unit Cost					Units Shipped			
	LA	SE	PH	Capacity		LA	SE	PH	Cost
LA-Reg	$1.13	$1.30	$1.24	420,000	LA-Reg	400,000		20,000	$476,800
LA-OT	$1.25	$1.42	$1.36	210,000	LA-OT			23,000	$31,280
SE-Reg	$1.25	$1.08	$1.28	300,000	SE-Reg		130,000	170,000	$358,000
SE-OT	$1.36	$1.19	$1.39	150,000	SE-OT				$0
					Required	400,000	130,000	213,000	
					Shortage	0	0	0	

Total Cost for Cluster 1 = $866,080

Cluster 2

	Unit Cost					Units Shipped			
	NY	DE	PI	Capacity		NY	DE	PI	Cost
NY-Reg	$1.12	$1.26	$1.20	490,000	NY-Reg	445,000		45,000	$552,400
NY-OT	$1.25	$1.39	$1.33	245,000	NY-OT				$0
DE-Reg	$1.20	$1.06	$1.18	370,000	DE-Reg		334,000	36,000	$396,520
DE-OT	$1.31	$1.17	$1.29	185,000	DE-OT			105,000	$135,450
					Required	445,000	334,000	186,000	
					Shortage	0	0	0	

Total Cost for Cluster 2 = $1,084,370

Cluster 3

	Unit Cost					Units Shipped			
	AT	KC	Capacity		AT	KC	Cost	Remaining Capacity
AT-Reg	$1.02	$1.17	340,000	AT-Reg	265,000	75,000	$358,050	0
AT-OT	$1.13	$1.28	170,000	AT-OT		65,000	$83,200	105,000
				Required	265,000	140,000		
				Shortage	0	0		

Total Cost for Cluster 3 = $441,250   Grand Total Cost = $2,391,700

EXHIBIT 28.7   Long Life Battery: Projected Demand at Distribution Centers

				Year				
Location	1	2	3	4	5	6	7	8
SE	130,000	132,600	135,252	137,957	140,716	143,531	146,401	149,329
LA	400,000	412,000	424,360	437,091	450,204	463,710	477,621	491,950
DE	334,000	337,340	340,713	344,121	347,562	351,037	354,548	358,093
NY	445,000	449,450	453,945	458,484	463,069	467,699	472,376	477,100
AT	265,000	270,300	275,706	281,220	286,845	292,581	298,433	304,402
PH	213,000	217,260	221,605	226,037	230,558	235,169	239,873	244,670
KC	140,000	142,800	145,656	148,569	151,541	154,571	157,663	160,816
PI	186,000	187,860	189,739	191,636	193,552	195,488	197,443	199,417

savings of $17,700 for next year, relative to the existing situation. These annual-cost savings sound like a promising return on a $100,000 investment. We consider the financial impact of making the $100,000 investment by computing the internal rate of return of annual cost savings that are associated with this initial capital outlay over the eight-year horizon for this project, after accounting for taxes and depreciation.

The analysis is complicated by the fact that different growth rates are associated with the different regions around the distribution centers. Exhibit 28.7 shows the projected annual demand values for each distribution center, using the growth rates from Exhibit 28.2. The least-total-annual-cost operating scenarios were determined by performing the calculations in Exhibit 28.5 with the existing case, for the projected demand values over each of the eight years in the project horizon. The same computations were also performed for each of the eight years in the project horizon following the format of Exhibit 28.6, with the New York expansion in place. The minimum-total-annual-cost values that were obtained for all of these cases are summarized in Exhibit 28.8.

Exhibit 28.9 then shows a summary of the financial analysis of operating with the associated cost savings from an expansion in New York over the eight-year time horizon of the project, accounting for the impact of taxes and depreciation of the $100,000 investment. The tax rate of 35% came for LLB personnel, and the depreciation schedule used in Exhibit 28.9 is the standard used by IRS for property of this life span. The net result is an internal rate

of return of 6.6% on the investment. While this internal rate of return for capacity expansion in New York is not particularly high, there are some additional significant nonmonetary benefits from reducing the continued reliance on excessive overtime.

A similar analysis was performed for a capacity expansion in Los Angeles. This analysis shows a reduction in operating cost over the eight years that corresponds to an internal rate of return of only 0.8%. This reduced internal rate of return is obtained despite the fact that LLB personnel have noted a substantially higher growth rate in Cluster 1 facilities (includes Los Angeles) than for Cluster 2 facilities (includes New York). We recommend expansion of the New York facility by 150,000 units per year of capacity.

EXHIBIT 28.8   Long Life Battery:
Minimum Total Annual Cost Values

Year	Existing Case	Expand NY
1	$2,409,400	$2,391,700
2	$2,454,652	$2,436,774
3	$2,500,841	$2,482,783
4	$2,547,988	$2,529,749
5	$2,596,118	$2,577,695
6	$2,645,247	$2,626,639
7	$2,695,409	$2,676,614
8	$2,746,722	$2,727,637

EXHIBIT 28.9 Long Life Battery: Financial Analysis for the Option of Expanding Capacity in New York

Year	Expense	Depreciation Percent	Depreciation Savings	Annual-Cost Savings	After-Tax Annual Cost	After-Tax Savings
0	$100,000	0	0	0	0	($100,000)
1	$0	14	$4,900	$17,700	$11,505	$16,405
2	$0	25	$8,750	$17,878	$11,621	$20,371
3	$0	17	$5,950	$18,058	$11,738	$17,688
4	$0	13	$4,550	$18,239	$11,855	$16,405
5	$0	9	$3,150	$18,423	$11,975	$15,125
6	$0	9	$3,150	$18,608	$12,095	$15,245
7	$0	9	$3,150	$18,795	$12,217	$15,367
8	$0	4	$1,400	$19,085	$12,405	$13,805
			$35,000			
Tax Rate =		0.35		IRR =		6.6%

FINAL RECOMMENDATIONS

In conclusion we recommend two actions for LLB:

- The cluster system should be implemented as a distribution policy. This requires no investment from LLB, and it will help contain shipping costs.

- A capacity increase of 150,000 units should be added to the New York facility. This will be helpful in reducing the firm's ongoing reliance on overtime. The internal rate of return is only 6.6%, but this option has some additional advantages, since an ongoing reliance on overtime can lead to employee burnout and to problems with quality issues.

Aggregate Scheduling

WVG, Inc.

WVG, Inc., is a large chemical company that produces many different types of end products for a number of different customers. Some of WVG's products have entered into the maturity phase of their life cycles, and WVG management is concerned about scheduling problems at one facility that produces some of these particular products. Demand for the specific products in question in this study can be expected to remain relatively stable for a number of years into the future, given the typical patterns of life cycles of related products.

The manager of the WVG facility that is being analyzed in this case is facing two problems. First, it is of interest to develop a cost-effective aggregate-production schedule for its two basic components, A and B, which are used in various mixes to produce a number of end products. A second issue is related to very significant problems that WVG has had with a subcontractor who can directly supply the facility with limited quantities of component A. These problems are of such a serious nature that the WVG manager wants to consider the option of expanding the existing storage facilities in order to be able to eliminate the need of having any reliance whatsoever on the outside supplier of Component A.

THE BASIC SITUATION

WVG manufactures both of two basic components, A and B, from a variety of raw materials at the plant at one of its facilities. There are no problems with obtaining any of the raw materials that are required to produce these components, as they are needed. Both A and B are very stable components that can be stored for extended periods with no problems. The WVG site has two towers that are used to store A and B. The towers are nearly identical, but once either A or B has been stored in a tower, it is a very costly process to clean that tower adequately to allow for the storage of the other component in the same tower. Therefore, one tower is always exclusively used for A and the other is always exclusively used for B.

This situation results from the fact that even though both of the individual components A and B are very stable components on their own, any mix of the two components becomes very unstable and must be sold for immediate use. The storage towers are identical except that any tower that is used to store component A must have a specialized venting system attached to it to neutralize vapors that would otherwise escape into the atmosphere. Since A and B have different densities, the capacity of a storage tower is different for A and B in terms of the weight of the component being stored. WVG measures all items in terms of thousands (1K) of pounds. One of the storage towers can hold 22.7K pounds of A or 12K pounds of B. There is a current inventory of 20.3K pounds of A and 9.7K pounds of B.

A mixing facility then combines components A and B in various proportions to produce three different end products: P1, P2, and P3. Different proportions of mixes of A and B can result in end products with very different characteristics. The mix of A and B in the three end products is given in Exhibit 29.1.

Projected demand for end products P1, P2, and P3 for the next seven months, as measured in thousands of pounds, is given in Exhibit 29.2. There is obviously some variability in the monthly demand for P1, P2, and P3. However, the schedule of predicted demand is typical of what can be expected throughout the year. The mixing facility operates with a small staff to produce P1, P2, and P3 as required by customers, and WVG is not experiencing any problems with the operation of the mixing facility.

The plant that produces components A and B is experiencing the first problem that is currently facing WVG management. The plant requires a crew of 25 workers to operate at any level of output. That is, the crew works as a team and all 25 workers are needed to operate the facility. Adjusting the number of workers that are being used cannot alter the hourly output of the facility, so that hiring of additional workers will not increase the hourly output of the facility. It is possible to let the facility be idle for short periods, and have a temporary layoff of the employees during the normal 160-hour work month, provided that the layoff does not take place for a significant portion of any month, or for any significant number of consecutive months.

Employees are paid at an average rate of $15 per hour per worker. Overtime work is possible, with a 50% premium on labor costs. However, there is a strict company policy that limits overtime work for employees to permit an additional 20 facility hours of operation per month. This policy exists because of quality and safety concerns if excessive overtime is used on a regular basis.

Monthly requirements for A and B are such that it is not possible to make just one run of A and one run of B during any month, without violating the storage capacity for

EXHIBIT 29.1
Mix of Components A and B in WVG End Products

Product	Percent A	Percent B
P1	80	20
P2	60	40
P3	50	50

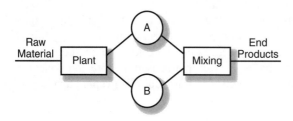

EXHIBIT 29.2
Demand
Forecasts for
WVG End
Products

	Product (1K Pounds)		
Month	P1	P2	P3
1	125	80	80
2	130	95	60
3	140	95	90
4	145	70	90
5	150	60	110
6	175	50	100
7	160	50	90

these components. It can be assumed that the manager of the production facility will continuously keep track of the existing quantities of each of the components that are in storage. Then the plant can frequently switch back and forth between the production of A and B during each month to meet the total monthly production requirements of each component, without running out of either, and without exceeding the capacity of the storage facilities.

The actual changeover cost for switching back and forth between the production of A and B at the plant is quite small, and it can be ignored as a component of the total cost. As a result of all of this, the amounts of A and B that are stored can be assumed to tend to generally increase, or decrease, throughout each given month. Inventory holding costs should therefore be assessed on the average monthly amounts of A and B that are held in inventory, and the average inventory values can be determined solely from the starting and ending monthly inventory quantities of each component. All of the problems with storing A and B that were mentioned above arise only after the two components have been mixed.

Holding costs are $750 per month for 1K pounds of A and $100 per month for 1K pounds of B. The large difference in holding costs results from the fact that there is a substantially lower cost for both raw materials and labor for producing component B. As stated before, there is nothing different between the storage facilities for A and B, other than the venting system that must be in place for component A, to cause this difference in the holding cost for each.

The plant must operate for .7 hours to produce 1K pounds of A, and for .3 hours to produce 1K pounds of B. It is impossible to produce A and B in the same plant at the same time due to the safety considerations discussed above. Scheduling in the plant is also made more difficult due to an inventory policy that must be maintained to prevent disruptions in the operation of the mixing facility. Because of time requirements to change the system over in the plant when switching the component that is being produced, and due to unexpected variation in demand, it is necessary to schedule production to have an ending inventory of both A and B at the end of each month that is at least 10% of the total forecasted requirement of each for the following month.

Greater actual demand than was forecasted during any given month might cause this policy to be violated, but scheduled production should meet the policy according to forecasted demand. Raw material costs are $4,000 per 1K pounds of A and $375 per 1K pounds of B. It is also possible to purchase up to 10K pounds of component A each month from an outside supplier at a cost of $7,000 per 1K pounds.

The manager of the WVG facility is concerned about how the aggregate schedule for the production of A and B has been developed in the past. A cost-effective schedule is desired for the next six months to minimize the combined cost of regular and overtime labor, raw material costs for A and B, holding costs for inventories of A and B, and the cost of purchasing A from the outside supplier. The schedule cannot account for output in month 7, since there are no forecasts for month 8 to fix the targeted ending inventory of components A and B for month 7. The total cost of the six-month schedule that is obtained can be assumed to represent the total costs for all six-month time increments.

SUPPLIER PROBLEMS

The second specific issue of interest concerns the serious difficulties that WVG management is having with the subcontractor who can be used as a source of component A. The manager of WVG is hoping that the economic-aggregate schedule that has just been developed will completely eliminate the need to rely on the subcontractor. There have been recurring problems with on-time deliveries from the subcontractor, and price increases have been incurred from the subcontractor on an almost monthly basis, while WVG has not observed any increase in raw-materials costs for producing A on its own.

There are no other practical sources of obtaining component A from any outside supplier. The manager of the WVG facility is extremely upset with the relationship with the subcontractor, that can best be defined as "extremely poor and getting worse." After many attempts to reconcile the issue, the manager of WVG sees no solution to the problem other than to produce all of component A within the WVG plant. The reliance of WVG on the subcontractor must be eliminated. If the cost-effective aggregate schedule that has just been obtained does not remove the reliance on the subcontractor, an alternative plan has been developed.

The alternative plan is to build a third storage tower that is identical to the existing tower for storing component A. The idea is to produce component A during slack production periods and then store it in the new tower to eliminate the need for buying the product from the subcontractor. The basic towers are similar to farm silos, so the size of the tower being considered is a standard size for a storage facility. The manager of WVG really wants to produce all of component A within the plant and is willing to accept this option with only a small return on investment, since continued price increases are expected from the subcontractor.

The cost of erecting the new storage facility for component A is $125,000. This cost consists of $100,000 for the basic silo and $25,000 for the specialized venting system needed if the silo is used to store component A. Once the venting system has been installed, there is no significant addition to operating cost from its being in place. The facility will be depreciated over eight years at annual rates of 14%, 25%, 17%, 13%, 9%, 9%, 9%, and 4% in successive years, and WVG pays taxes at a rate of 35%. There must be some resulting savings in total annual operating costs if the third storage facility is added to the operation. The manager of WVG is interested in knowing the internal rate of return of this flow of annual cost savings, accounting for depreciation and taxation, over the eight-year horizon, with the $125,000 initial expense being invested immediately. All other costs and savings would be evaluated at the end of each year in the horizon.

Of immediate interest is the internal rate of return that would be obtained by building the additional storage tower. It would be particularly useful to the manager if a much better solution to this problem could be found that completely removes WVG's dependence on the subcontractor.

Mooselook Boat Company

Mooselook Boat Company (MBC) is located in Bemis, Maine, in the western mountain region of that state. MBC is a small manufacturer of wooden canoes, and it has been operating profitably since it was started in the 1930s. The company was originally formed to produce high-quality boats for use by local fishermen, and for the owners of fairly rustic summer camps that were being developed around regional lakes at that time. Due to changes in the demographics of the customer base in the region, MBC started to specialize in the production of high-quality wooden canoes some years ago and it has been a very successful business. The change in the customer base resulted from a significant increase in the number of part-time residents who spend summers in the region. These customers are mostly interested in having canoes for general recreational purposes, rather than in having a boat to use for fishing. The part-time residents typically are on the high end of the family income spectrum, and they have been willing to pay a significantly higher price for the aesthetics of wooden canoes, compared to the option of buying relatively inexpensive aluminum canoes.

The dramatic increase in the development of western Maine over the years led to a significant increase in demand for wooden canoes from part-time residents. Also, as the highway system and infrastructure became greatly improved in the area, it became more feasible for MBC to expand its distribution over a significantly larger area. As a result of the increase in demand, MBC built a new production facility adjacent to the original production facility in 1985, but it did not get rid of the original production facility. The new production facility was also established to account for the fact that the level of general carpentry skills was declining among local employees due to changes in vocational training in the secondary school system. Thus, the new production facility was based on a much more mechanized procedure for building wooden canoes. By using a series of forms and specially designed clamps, it is possible to construct the canoes in significantly less time in the new facility, while allowing for the reduced carpentry skills of employees.

Local workers have historically assembled the wooden canoes during the winter season, with a production period that runs from January through June. This part-year production schedule serves two purposes. First, it allows MBC to be in operation during the peak requirements periods of the highly seasonal demand cycle. Second, it allows workers to engage in other seasonal employment during the off period, such as working in the logging industry or being engaged in local service businesses that are geared toward the part-time summer residents. The people who live in the region around Bemis are now very dependent on income generated by visitors during the summer and fall seasons, so MBC employees still require the same seasonal work schedule. As a result, the January through June work schedule must be continued.

CAPACITIES

The original production facility was left intact and it can easily be put back into operation without incurring any significant start-up cost whenever demand warrants it. Moving experienced employees from the new production facility to the old facility and replacing them in the new production facility with temporary help can accomplish this goal. The capacity of the old production facility is 100 canoes per month, and it takes an average of 20 employee work-hours to construct a canoe by the old process. Due to inefficiencies in the old process, there is a 60% premium on unit overtime labor costs. The overtime production capacity of the old facility is only 20 canoes per month.

The new production facility has a capacity of 400 canoes per month with the possible addition of 100 canoes per month on overtime. It only takes an average of 16 employee work-hours to produce a canoe with the new production process, and there is a 50% premium on unit overtime labor costs. The same amount of material is required to build a canoe by either of these two processes. Employees who work as canoe builders at MBC receive total compensation at an average rate of $12 per hour for regular-time work.

INVENTORY

After each canoe is produced, a wooden frame is built around it to allow for stacking during storage. MBC had a warehouse near the new production facility, but it burned down several years ago. Since that time, canoes have been stored in three barns that belong to the owner of MBC. These barns are located in Houghton, about 15 miles from the production facility, and the average cost of storing a canoe at one of these barns is $56 per month. This cost might seem quite high, but it is based largely on the sizeable investment that MBC must make in raw materials and labor to produce a canoe before it goes to storage. This investment is gaining no return for MBC as the canoes just sit in inventory. If production exceeds demand in any given month, the excess tends to build up in inventory at a constant rate. The inventory also tends to decline at a constant rate when demand exceeds production in any month. As a result, holding costs should be assessed on the average number of units that are held in inventory during each month. The maximum inventory capacity is 800 canoes.

A number of competing companies can supply a comparable product at about the same price as MBC. It is therefore important to be assured that we can meet orders soon after they are received. The company has adopted two different inventory policies in order to be assured that incoming orders can be met quickly. The first policy applies to the end of every month during the January-to-June production cycle, when most demand is observed. There should be sufficient inventory at the end of each of these months to meet 125 percent of forecasted demand during the following month.

The inventory on hand at the end of June must also be sufficient to meet expected orders during the rest of the year. To be assured that inventory can cover variations in forecasted demand during the nonproduction part of the year, the second policy requires that the inventory on hand at the end of June should be sufficient to meet 125 percent of the total forecasted demand for the period of July through December. There is sufficient variability in demand to make forecasting difficult. This forecasting difficulty, coupled with heavy competition, makes MBC's owner insistent upon continuing these two inventory policies.

DEMAND

There is obviously a highly seasonal nature to the demand for wooden canoes. A basic underlying demand for about 100 canoes per month exists year round. Canoes that are shipped to southern states typically account for most of this demand. A peak in demand occurs between March and June as dealers in the New England area increase their inventory levels to be ready for spring and summer business. Monthly demand for the upcoming year has been forecasted, and the results are shown in Exhibit 30.1.

SCHEDULING

The start of a new production year is approaching and the owner of MBC is attempting to determine an overall plan for scheduling production in order to meet forecasted demand. The owner is interested in knowing if the old production facility will be needed to meet demand while meeting the two inventory policies. At the beginning of the current production year, approximately 150 canoes will remain in inventory.

The cost of raw materials is a major component of the total cost of building these wooden canoes. All competing canoe builders will be forced to modify their prices as the costs of raw materials change, but all builders are paying comparable prices for these raw materials. In any event, the cost of raw materials is not really relevant to determining the timing of the optimal scheduling policy for MBC, so it will be ignored when determining a least-total-cost schedule. The cost of materials is considered indirectly, as it applies to inventory holding costs for storing finished canoes, as discussed above. The scheduling policy should specifically state the anticipated monthly regular and overtime production for each of the production facilities, and it should also state the anticipated inventory level at the end of each month. This production-inventory schedule should minimize the total cost of production and storage.

EXHIBIT 30.1
Monthly Demand Forecasts for MBC Canoes

Month	Demand
January	100
February	100
March	300
April	460
May	500
June	400
July	100
August	100
September	100
October	100
November	100
December	100

ADDITIONAL PROBLEMS

The owner of MBC is also facing some long-range problems. Over recent years, the total overall demand for high-quality wooden canoes has reached a plateau, and it is expected to continue at this level over the near future. However, the long-term demand for high-quality wooden canoes is not promising. Consumer demand for high-quality canoes is shifting toward canoes that are made out of composite materials. These canoes are extremely light for portaging and they are extremely durable. The process technology for producing composite canoes would also remove MBC's reliance on carpentry skills from employees. The owner of MBC is therefore interested in getting out of the wooden canoe business when the current production facilities are no longer usable. It is expected that the new production facility will remain useful for eight more years.

In eight years, the owner wants to quit the wooden canoe business and build a new production facility to produce canoes from composite materials. The demand for wooden canoes is expected to start declining slowly at some point during the eight-year period. None of the wooden canoe production facilities will be of any use whatsoever in building composite material canoes, since the manufacturing processes for wooden and composite material canoes are completely different.

A cabinet shop is also being opened in Summit, several miles from Bemis, and the owner of MBC has been offered $150,000 for all of the woodworking equipment in the old production facility. The cabinet shop could never use the equipment to produce wooden canoes to compete with MBC. This equipment has already been fully depreciated, and MBC is paying taxes at a rate of 35 percent. The owner of MBC would be interested in closing down the old production facility if the $150,000 sale will offset the after-tax increase in production and inventory costs that result from operating without the old production facility. The owner of MBC also wants to know exactly how the closing of the old production facility would alter the production-inventory schedule. If the old production facility is only used infrequently, the equipment in it can be expected to maintain about one-fourth of its current sale value after eight years, since the equipment is general-purpose woodworking equipment that has many possible uses in specialty woodworking applications.

If the owner decides to sell the equipment in the old production facility, the structure of the old facility could be demolished and be replaced by a new temporary storage facility. This new storage facility would cost $450,000 and it would provide storage for 800 canoes. This temporary storage facility would last for eight years, until the conversion to composite material canoe production will take place, but it will be of no value after the conversion takes place. One major reason for considering this new storage facility is that it would be located much nearer the production facility and would reduce the current inventory storage costs by 25 percent. The depreciation of the temporary storage facility would take place over eight years (14%, 25%, 17%, 13%, 9%, 9%, 9%, 4%).

If the owner of MBC does not build the temporary storage facility, MBC must incur a maintenance expense for the currently used storage barns, without regard to the decision about selling the equipment in the old production facility. The estimated one-time total cost for maintenance of the three barns is $24,000. The maintenance would not actually prolong the life of the storage barns, so the expense could be deducted during the current year. If the new storage facility were to be built, there would be no need for maintenance of the storage barns, since they would no longer be used.

The owner of MBC wants to know how the construction of the new storage facility would affect the production-inventory schedule. Since capital is already being accumulated to pay for the conversion to composite material canoe production and since demand is not completely certain in the future, the owner would only consider building the new storage facility if it were clearly superior to the option of using the current storage facilities.

SUMMARY

There are three options that are available to the owner of MBC:

- Option 1: Continue with the existing situation for eight years, and perform maintenance on the barn roofs.
- Option 2: Sell the equipment in the old production facility and operate without it for eight years. This would require maintenance on the barn roofs.
- Option 3: Sell the equipment in the old production facility, build a new storage facility, and operate for the next eight years. This option would not require maintenance of the barn roofs.

Due to the level of uncertainty about the future, the owner of MBC is reluctant to make any changes to the existing situation. Answers to the following questions would be of great help to the owner.

- At what discount rate do we have equality of the net present values of the eight-year stream of after-tax and depreciation costs for Option 1 and Option 2?
- At what discount rate do we have equality of the net present values of the eight-year stream of after-tax and depreciation costs for Option 2 and Option 3?
- What else can be done to help in the decision process?

In performing the net present value computations, we should associate all operating costs, revenues from equipment sales, tax savings from depreciation, and barn maintenance costs with payments at the end of their respective years. However, the cost for building the new storage facility would be incurred immediately if Option 3 were to be selected.

Lenin Toy Company

Lenin Toy Company (LTC) produces a national line of toys for children. The company has been very successful over many years with a number of different products, and it currently has manufacturing facilities established in many different locations. The production facility of particular interest in this case is located in Erie, Pennsylvania. The Erie plant is the main producer of one of LTC's principal toy specialties, the Wonder Wheel. The Wonder Wheel consists of a heavy-gauge plastic circular frame with three wheels attached. A child sits in a seat that is molded into the frame and can maneuver the Wonder Wheel in many different directions by working a set of pedals and hand cranks.

LTC is very familiar with the demand growth curve for all kinds of toys, and the Wonder Wheel has clearly reached a sales plateau in its maturity phase, where it should have relatively stable demand for six or seven years, after which sales can be expected to start declining. All toys have a highly seasonal demand, with peaks in retail sales occurring just before Christmas. This leads to peaks in demand for LTC that occur a few months before Christmas when they are making shipments to wholesale distributors.

Exhibit 31.1 shows the forecasted monthly demand for Wonder Wheels during the upcoming sales year. The demand forecasts in Exhibit 31.1 should be quite accurate due to the extensive previous experience of the firm, the fact that toy sales tend to be "recession proof," and a series of patents that are held by LTC to protect the design of Wonder Wheels.

EXHIBIT 31.1
Forecasted
Monthly
Demand,
and Modified
Monthly
Demand,
for Wonder
Wheels

Month	Expected Demand	Modified Demand
January	9,000	9,000
February	9,000	9,000
March	10,000	10,000
April	10,000	10,000
May	12,000	42,000
June	15,000	65,000
July	40,000	80,000
August	140,000	80,000
September	190,000	130,000
October	80,000	80,000
November	60,000	60,000
December	25,000	25,000

PRODUCTION—INVENTORY PROCESS

The Erie Plant of LTC is split into two parts. The 18th Street plant originally housed the entire production and inventory storage facility. Some years ago, significantly increased production requirements for Wonder Wheels forced the purchase of a building on 12th Street that LTC now uses for an inventory storage site. The 18th Street plant is completely surrounded by other facilities that are owned by other companies, so it was therefore impossible to have any significant expansion of the total size of the base plant on 18th Street when the production capacity was increased at that time. The 12th Street site was a vacant existing facility that was purchased at a good price and allowed LTC to avoid the prohibitive expense of rebuilding an entire production facility at another location. However, the distance between the two facilities does lead to increased costs in getting finished product to the storage site. The size of the 12th Street plant limits maximum inventory capacity to 150,000 Wonder Wheels.

Shipments of the assembled product to distributors can take place in two ways. First, tractor-trailers can back up to a loading dock at the 18th Street plant and have direct shipment to distributors. Common carriers are used in this situation to haul the Wonder Wheels directly to distributors, without ever sending finished product to LTC inventory. If items are going to LTC inventory for storage, another process is used.

LTC uses its own trucks to haul the completed items to the 12th Street facility for inventory storage if they are not directly shipped from the 18th Street plant. This extra step causes increased handling and packing requirements for items that are sent to inventory storage. It is estimated that it costs an additional $.44 per unit to move a Wonder Wheel to its position in storage. When items are later removed from inventory and are placed on a common carrier for shipment to distributors, an additional cost of $.36 per unit is incurred. Neither of these additional handling costs is applicable to units that go out by direct shipment from the 18th Street plant. Once a unit is loaded on a common carrier for final delivery to distributors, the shipping cost is the same regardless of whether it is shipped directly or from inventory. The variable inventory holding cost is $.40 per unit each month.

In months when production output is greater than demand, inventory tends to build up at a fairly constant rate during that month. When demand exceeds production in any month, then inventory tends to decline at a fairly constant rate during that month. As a result of all of this, costs for holding inventory should be assessed on the average number of units that are held in inventory in any given month. Moreover, the average monthly inventory in any given month can be obtained directly as the average of the starting and ending inventory levels for that month.

All plastic casting of Wonder Wheel components is subcontracted to outside firms in the area, and the 18th Street production facility is primarily involved in the assembly of these components. Due to the highly seasonal nature of demand, one of LTC's major problems is scheduling the size of its work force. LTC hires most of its employees in the spring and puts them on layoff after the peak of the season has passed. This hire-layoff process has been done somewhat haphazardly in the past on an as-needed basis. However, the repeated hire-layoff process does not cause any serious problem with the employees. The typical worker at LTC is a second-income earner in their family who does not really want a full-time job on a year-round basis and is not disturbed by the layoff period every year. Overall relations between LTC and their employees are quite good.

When employees are hired, they must be given a physical exam and be issued some safety equipment. These hiring costs, along with other paperwork costs, amount to $790 every time an employee is either hired or rehired. Similarly, when an employee is laid off, a cost of $570 is incurred for processing. The assembly jobs at LTC are of such a nature that a typical employee can be trained to do most of the jobs very quickly. The average employee costs LTC about $2,120 per month, part of which is the employer's contribution to social security, unemployment compensation, retirement fund, and other miscellaneous expenses. All hiring and layoffs take place at the start of each month.

The actual assembly process at LTC takes place at a set of benches. Each assembler works at a bench and constructs a complete Wonder Wheel from components that pass overhead on a set of hooks that are moving on a guided chain. Each assembler works independently while producing Wonder Wheels, and they also package the finished item. The firm employs this production process for two reasons. First, the employees find it less boring to assemble a complete Wonder Wheel than having the process run like a standard assembly line. Second, adding or removing workers from benches can then be used to modify the production rate easily and effectively. There currently are 20 benches in the 18th Street plant, and any number of these benches can be staffed and used. The average LTC worker can assemble 4,000 Wonder Wheels in a month, while working a standard eight-hour shift each day. The process can be operated on an overtime basis, with an overtime capacity of up to 50% of the regular shift capacity. There is a standard 50% premium on all employee costs when they are working on an overtime basis. It is not feasible to initiate a second shift due to a limited availability of supervisory personnel.

PROBLEMS

The manager of LTC in Erie is concerned about meeting the projected demand for Wonder Wheels since the demand has settled at a plateau that is greater than what it was expected to be when the 18th Street plant was converted to produce Wonder Wheels. Two ideas have been developed to cope with this problem. The first idea is to attack the problem directly by extending the production facility into a relatively small storage room, which could be eliminated. This would entail knocking down a wall, making some structural modifications to the building, and setting up new assembly benches in the space that would be made available.

These new benches would essentially be identical to the old benches, and the available space that would be created would allow for an increase in the maximum staffing capacity by up to 25% beyond the existing 20 benches. That is, LTC would have the option of adding 1, 2, 3, 4, or 5 benches. The basic idea is to gear production more directly to demand, which thereby helps save some of the high inventory costs by allowing the use of more direct shipments. The total cost of this project would require a one-time fixed cost of $35,000 to perform the initial structural modifications to the building, and an additional one-time cost of $35,000 for each additional bench that is set up in the new space. The total cost for setting up these additional benches would be incurred immediately, and the associated capital expense would be depreciated over six years at standard rates (20%, 32%, 19%, 12%, 11%, 6%).

The second possible option is to deal with the problem indirectly, by trying to smooth out the peaks in demand. Offering price breaks to distributors who place orders early, when demand is relatively low, could accomplish this goal. Under this cost reduction plan, the basic factory unit price of $24 to distributors would be cut by 4.5 percent for all May orders, 3% for all June orders and 1.5% for all July orders. The LTC marketing department has predicted that these discounts would shift the original forecasted demand estimates without price reductions to the modified demand estimates that are shown in Exhibit 31.1. Since the price cuts are not that large, and since the product is somewhat unique, the price cuts would not result in any significant increase in total demand for the product. Of course, LTC would actually ship all orders in the month that the distributors placed them with this price reduction option, or there would be no real resulting saving in total operating costs. This option might be appealing to LTC if the reduction in total operating cost would offset the resulting lost revenues from giving the price breaks.

The manager of the LTC plant in Erie is having difficulty in determining the ultimate impact that each of these options would have on production-inventory work force planning. It is possible to use either, or both, of the options. With the expansion option, the decision is also open to add 1, 2, 3, 4, or 5 new benches. The decision horizon for this project is six years. The manager of LTC wants to see a summary of the net present value of all costs, after accounting for tax and depreciation, for every possible option that is available for consideration. All costs and tax savings from depreciation should be discounted at the end of the respective years that they occur. However, all expenses that are associated with any expansion option should be taken as an immediate expense, with no discounting. LTC pays taxes at a rate of 35% and it uses a discount factor of 12% when performing net present value analysis. The manager also wants any additional input that might have an impact on the determination of the option that should ultimately be selected, beyond the basic summary of all of the net present value.*

*Technical note: In doing this case, you are not given the starting number of workers or the existing level of inventory. Given the nature of the business, it would be expected that both would be very low going into January. Obtain a solution to minimize the total cost for a one-year cycle with the starting inventory and number of workers being whatever they should be to allow for a smooth transition from year to year. For example, the starting inventory in January would simply be defined to be the same as the ending inventory from December. The same logic would hold for the number of workers. In all financial analysis, the same identical cycle would then be assumed to repeat itself over each of the years in the six-year horizon. In addition, since all hiring and layoff takes place at the start of each month, the number of workers in each month must be integer valued.